The Poetry of Alan Seege

Alan Seeger was born on June 22nd 1888 in New York. The family moved to Staten Island when he was 1 for 9 years and then on to Mexico until he was 12. After attending several elite preparatory schools he enrolled at Harvard in 1906 where he also edited and wrote for the Harvard Monthly.

He graduated in 1910 and went to live the life of a bohemian in Greenwich Village, New York thereafter moving to Paris to continue his poetry writing in the Latin quarter.

War's looming dark shadow was to have a transformative effect on the young poet and on August 24th 1914 he joined the French Foreign Legion so he could fight for the Allies.

On American Independence day, July 4th, 1917 whilst urging on his fellow soldiers in a successful charge at Belloy-en-Santerre he was hit several times by machine gun fire and died.

His poetry was published posthumously later that year, it was not a great success but his poem 'I Have a Rendezvous with Death . . .' is now regarded as a classic.

On the sixth anniversary of his death a memorial to the American volunteers was unveiled in the Place des Etats-Unis. The memorial was created by Jean Boucher who had used a photograph of Seeger as his inspiration. Two quotes from his poem 'Ode in Memory of the American Volunteers Fallen for France are inscribed upon it: "They did not pursue worldly rewards; they wanted nothing more than to live without regret, brothers pledged to the honour implicit in living one's own life and dying one's own death. Hail, brothers! Goodbye to you, the exalted dead! To you, we owe two debts of gratitude forever: the glory of having died for France, and the homage due to you in our memories."

Index Of Poems

Juvenilia

1914

An Ode to Natural Beauty
There is a power whose inspiration fills
Nature's fair fabric, sun-and star-inwrought,
Like airy dew ere any drop distils,
Like perfume in the laden flower, like aught
Unseen which interfused throughout the whole
Becomes its quickening pulse and principle and soul.
Now when, the drift of old desire renewing,
Warm tides flow northward over valley and field,
When half-forgotten sound and scent are wooing
From their deep-chambered recesses long sealed
Such memories as breathe once more
Of childhood and the happy hues it wore,
Now, with a fervor that has never been
In years gone by, it stirs me to respond,
Not as a force whose fountains are within
The faculties of the percipient mind,
Subject with them to darkness and decay,
But something absolute, something beyond,
Oft met like tender orbs that seem to peer
From pale horizons, luminous behind
Some fringe of tinted cloud at close of day;
And in this flood of the reviving year,
When to the loiterer by sylvan streams,
Deep in those cares that make Youth loveliest,
Nature in every common aspect seems
To comment on the burden in his breast
The joys he covets and the dreams he dreams

One then with all beneath the radiant skies
That laughs with him or sighs,
It courses through the lilac-scented air,
A blessing on the fields, a wonder everywhere.

Spirit of Beauty, whose sweet impulses,
Flung like the rose of dawn across the sea,
Alone can flush the exalted consciousness
With shafts of sensible divinity
Light of the World, essential loveliness:
Him whom the Muse hath made thy votary
Not from her paths and gentle preceptture
Shall vulgar ends engage, nor break the spell
That taught him first to feel thy secret charms
And o'er the earth, obedient to their lure,
Their sweet surprise and endless miracle,
To follow ever with insatiate arms.
On summer afternoons,
When from the blue horizon to the shore,
Casting faint silver pathways like the moon's
Across the Ocean's glassy, mottled floor,
Far clouds uprear their gleaming battlements
Drawn to the crest of some bleak eminence,
When autumn twilight fades on the sere hill
And autumn winds are still;
To watch the East for some emerging sign,
Wintry Capella or the Pleiades
Or that great huntsman with the golden gear;
Ravished in hours like these
Before thy universal shrine
To feel the invoked presence hovering near,
He stands enthusiastic. Star-lit hours
Spent on the roads of wandering solitude
Have set their sober impress on his brow,
And he, with harmonies of wind and wood
And torrent and the tread of mountain showers,
Has mingled many a dedicative vow
That holds him, till thy last delight be known,
Bound in thy service and in thine alone.

I, too, among the visionary throng
Who choose to follow where thy pathway leads,
Have sold my patrimony for a song,
And donned the simple, lowly pilgrim's weeds.
From that first image of beloved walls,
Deep-bowered in umbrage of ancestral trees,
Where earliest thy sweet enchantment falls,
Tingeing a child's fantastic reveries
With radiance so fair it seems to be
Of heavens just lost the lingering evidence
From that first dawn of roseate infancy,

So long beneath thy tender influence
My breast has thrilled. As oft for one brief second
The veil through which those infinite offers beckoned
Has seemed to tremble, letting through
Some swift intolerable view
Of vistas past the sense of mortal seeing,
So oft, as one whose stricken eyes might see
In ferny dells the rustic deity,
I stood, like him, possessed, and all my being,
Flooded an instant with unwonted light,
Quivered with cosmic passion; whether then
On woody pass or glistening mountain-height
I walked in fellowship with winds and clouds,
Whether in cities and the throngs of men,
A curious saunterer through friendly crowds,
Enamored of the glance in passing eyes,
Unuttered salutations, mute replies,
In every character where light of thine
Has shed on earthly things the hue of things divine
I sought eternal Loveliness, and seeking,
If ever transport crossed my brow bespeaking
Such fire as a prophetic heart might feel
Where simple worship blends in fervent zeal,
It was the faith that only love of thee
Needed in human hearts for Earth to see
Surpassed the vision poets have held dear
Of joy diffused in most communion here;
That whomsoe'er thy visitations warmed,
Lover of thee in all thy rays informed,
Needed no difficulter discipline
To seek his right to happiness within
Than, sensible of Nature's loveliness,
To yield him to the generous impulses
By such a sentiment evoked. The thought,
Bright Spirit, whose illuminings I sought,
That thou unto thy worshipper might be
An all-sufficient law, abode with me,
Importing something more than unsubstantial dreams
To vigils by lone shores and walks by murmuring streams.

Youth's flowers like childhood's fade and are forgot.
Fame twines a tardy crown of yellowing leaves.
How swift were disillusion, were it not
That thou art steadfast where all else deceives!
Solace and Inspiration, Power divine
That by some mystic sympathy of thine,
When least it waits and most hath need of thee,
Can startle the dull spirit suddenly
With grandeur welled from unsuspected springs,
Long as the light of fulgent evenings,
When from warm showers the pearly shades disband

And sunset opens o'er the humid land,
Shows thy veiled immanence in orient skies,
Long as pale mist and opalescent dyes
Hung on far isle or vanishing mountain-crest,
Fields of remote enchantment can suggest
So sweet to wander in it matters nought,
They hold no place but in impassioned thought,
Long as one draught from a clear sky may be
A scented luxury;
Be thou my worship, thou my sole desire,
Thy paths my pilgrimage, my sense a lyre
Aeolian for thine every breath to stir;
Oft when her full-blown periods recur,
To see the birth of day's transparent moon
Far from cramped walls may fading afternoon
Find me expectant on some rising lawn;
Often depressed in dewy grass at dawn,
Me, from sweet slumber underneath green boughs,
Ere the stars flee may forest matins rouse,
Afoot when the great sun in amber floods
Pours horizontal through the steaming woods
And windless fumes from early chimneys start
And many a cock-crow cheers the traveller's heart
Eager for aught the coming day afford
In hills untopped and valleys unexplored.
Give me the white road into the world's ends,
Lover of roadside hazard, roadside friends,
Loiterer oft by upland farms to gaze
On ample prospects, lost in glimmering haze
At noon, or where down odorous dales twilit,
Filled with low thundering of the mountain stream,
Over the plain where blue seas border it
The torrid coast-towns gleam.

I have fared too far to turn back now; my breast
Burns with the lust for splendors unrevealed,
Stars of midsummer, clouds out of the west,
Pallid horizons, winds that valley and field
Laden with joy, be ye my refuge still!
What though distress and poverty assail!
Though other voices chide, yours never will.
The grace of a blue sky can never fail.
Powers that my childhood with a spell so sweet,
My youth with visions of such glory nursed,
Ye have beheld, nor ever seen my feet
On any venture set, but 'twas the thirst
For Beauty willed them, yea, whatever be
The faults I wanted wings to rise above;
I am cheered yet to think how steadfastly
I have been loyal to the love of Love!

The Deserted Garden
I know a village in a far-off land
Where from a sunny, mountain-girdled plain
With tinted walls a space on either hand
And fed by many an olive-darkened lane
The high-road mounts, and thence a silver band
Through vineyard slopes above and rolling grain,
Winds off to that dim corner of the skies
Where behind sunset hills a stately city lies.

Here, among trees whose overhanging shade
Strews petals on the little droves below,
Pattering townward in the morning weighed
With greens from many an upland garden-row,
Runs an old wall; long centuries have frayed
Its scalloped edge, and passers to and fro
Heard never from beyond its crumbling height
Sweet laughter ring at noon or plaintive song at night.

But here where little lizards bask and blink
The tendrils of the trumpet-vine have run,
At whose red bells the humming bird to drink
Stops oft before his garden feast is done;
And rose-geraniums, with that tender pink
That cloud-banks borrow from the setting sun,
Have covered part of this old wall, entwined
With fair plumbago, blue as evening heavens behind.

And crowning other parts the wild white rose
Rivals the honey-suckle with the bees.
Above the old abandoned orchard shows
And all within beneath the dense-set trees,
Tall and luxuriant the rank grass grows,
That settled in its wavy depth one sees
Grass melt in leaves, the mossy trunks between,
Down fading avenues of implicated green;

Wherein no lack of flowers the verdurous night
With stars and pearly nebula o'erlay;
Azalea-boughs half rosy and half white
Shine through the green and clustering apple-spray,
Such as the fairy-queen before her knight
Waved in old story, luring him away
Where round lost isles Hesperian billows break
Or towers loom up beneath the clear, translucent lake;

And under the deep grass blue hare-bells hide,
And myrtle plots with dew-fall ever wet,
Gay tiger-lilies flammulate and pied,
Sometime on pathway borders neatly set,

Now blossom through the brake on either side,
Where heliotrope and weedy mignonette,
With vines in bloom and flower-bearing trees,
Mingle their incense all to swell the perfumed breeze,

That sprung like Hermes from his natal cave
In some blue rampart of the curving West,
Comes up the valleys where green cornfields wave,
Ravels the cloud about the mountain crest,
Breathes on the lake till gentle ripples pave
Its placid floor; at length a long-loved guest,
He steals across this plot of pleasant ground,
Waking the vocal leaves to a sweet vernal sound.

Here many a day right gladly have I sped,
Content amid the wavy plumes to lie,
And through the woven branches overhead
Watch the white, ever-wandering clouds go by,
And soaring birds make their dissolving bed
Far in the azure depths of summer sky,
Or nearer that small huntsman of the air,
The fly-catcher, dart nimbly from his leafy lair;

Pillowed at ease to hear the merry tune
Of mating warblers in the boughs above
And shrill cicadas whom the hottest noon
Keeps not from drowsy song; the mourning dove
Pours down the murmuring grove his plaintive croon
That like the voice of visionary love
Oft have I risen to seek through this green maze
(Even as my feet thread now the great world's garden-ways);

And, parting tangled bushes as I passed
Down beechen alleys beautiful and dim,
Perhaps by some deep-shaded pool at last
My feet would pause, where goldfish poise and swim,
And snowy callas' velvet cups are massed
Around the mossy, fern-encircled brim.
Here, then, that magic summoning would cease,
Or sound far off again among the orchard trees.

And here where the blanched lilies of the vale
And violets and yellow star-flowers teem,
And pink and purple hyacinths exhale
Their heavy fume, once more to drowse and dream
My head would sink, from many an olden tale
Drawing imagination's fervid theme,
Or haply peopling this enchanting spot
Only with fair creations of fantastic thought.

For oft I think, in years long since gone by,

That gentle hearts dwelt here and gentle hands
Stored all this bowery bliss to beautify
The paradise of some unsung romance;
Here, safe from all except the loved one's eye,
'Tis sweet to think white limbs were wont to glance,
Well pleased to wanton like the flowers and share
Their simple loveliness with the enamored air.

Thrice dear to them whose votive fingers decked
The altars of First Love were these green ways,
These lawns and verdurous brakes forever flecked
With the warm sunshine of midsummer days;
Oft where the long straight allies intersect
And marble seats surround the open space,
Where a tiled pool and sculptured fountain stand,
Hath Evening found them seated, silent, hand in hand.

When twilight deepened, in the gathering shade
Beneath that old titanic cypress row,
Whose sombre vault and towering colonnade
Dwarfed the enfolded forms that moved below,
Oft with close steps these happy lovers strayed,
Till down its darkening aisle the sunset glow
Grew less and patterning the garden floor
Faint flakes of filtering moonlight mantled more and more.

And the strange tempest that a touch imparts
Through the mid fibre of the molten frame,
When the sweet flesh in early youth asserts
Its heyday verve and little hints enflame,
Disturbed them as they walked; from their full hearts
Welled the soft word, and many a tender name
Strove on their lips as breast to breast they strained
And the deep joy they drank seemed never, never drained.

Love's soul that is the depth of starry skies
Set in the splendor of one upturned face
To beam adorably through half-closed eyes;
Love's body where the breadth of summer days
And all the beauty earth and air comprise
Come to the compass of an arm's embrace,
To burn a moment on impassioned lips
And yield intemperate joy to quivering finger-tips,

They knew; and here where morning-glories cling
Round carven forms of carefullest artifice,
They made a bower where every outward thing
Should comment on the cause of their own bliss;
With flowers of liveliest hue encompassing
That flower that the beloved body is
That rose that for the banquet of Love's bee

Has budded all the aeons of past eternity.

But their choice seat was where the garden wall,
Crowning a little summit, far and near,
Looks over tufted treetops onto all
The pleasant outer country; rising here
From rustling foliage where cuckoos call
On summer evenings, stands a belvedere,
Buff-hued, of antique plaster, overrun
With flowering vines and weatherworn by rain and sun.

Still round the turrets of this antique tower
The bougainvillea hangs a crimson crown,
Wistaria-vines and clematis in flower,
Wreathing the lower surface further down,
Hide the old plaster in a very shower
Of motley blossoms like a broidered gown.
Outside, ascending from the garden grove,
A crumbling stairway winds to the one room above.

And whoso mounts by this dismantled stair
Finds the old pleasure-hall, long disarrayed,
Brick-tiled and raftered, and the walls foursquare
Ringed all about with a twofold arcade.
Backward dense branches intercept the glare
Of afternoon with eucalyptus shade;
Eastward the level valley-plains expand,
Sweet as a queen's survey of her own Fairyland.

For through that frame the ivied arches make,
Wide tracts of sunny midland charm the eye,
Frequent with hamlet, grove, and lucent lake
Where the blue hills' inverted contours lie;
Far to the east where billowy mountains break
In surf of snow against a sapphire sky,
Huge thunderheads loom up behind the ranges,
Changing from gold to pink as deepening sunset changes;

And over plain and far sierra spread
The fulgent rays of fading afternoon,
Showing each utmost peak and watershed
All clarified, each tassel and festoon
Of floating cloud embroidered overhead,
Like lotus-leaves on bluest waters strewn,
Flushing with rose, while all breathes fresh and free
In peace and amplitude and bland tranquillity.

Dear were such evenings to this gentle pair;
Love's tide that launched on with a blast too strong
Sweeps toward the foaming reef, the hidden snare,
Baffling with fond illusion's siren-song,

Too faint, on idle shoals, to linger there
Far from Youth's glowing dream, bore them along,
With purple sail and steered by seraph hands
To isles resplendent in the sunset of romance.

And out of this old house a flowery fane,
A bridal bower, a pearly pleasure-dome,
They built, and furnished it with gold and grain,
And bade all spirits of beauty hither come,
And winged Love to enter with his train
And bless their pillow, and in this his home
Make them his priests as Hero was of yore
In her sweet girlhood by the blue Dardanian shore.

Tree-ferns, therefore, and potted palms they brought,
Tripods and urns in rare and curious taste,
Polychrome chests and cabinets inwrought
With pearl and ivory etched and interlaced;
Pendant brocades with massive braid were caught,
And chain-slung, oriental lamps so placed
To light the lounger on some low divan,
Sunken in swelling down and silks from Hindustan.

And there was spread, upon the ample floors,
Work of the Levantine's laborious loom,
Such as by Euxine or Ionian shores
Carpets the dim seraglio's scented gloom.
Each morn renewed, the garden's flowery stores
Blushed in fair vases, ochre and peach-bloom,
And little birds through wicker doors left wide
Flew in to trill a space from the green world outside.

And there was many a dainty attitude,
Bronze and eburnean. All but disarrayed,
Here in eternal doubt sweet Psyche stood
Fain of the bath's delight, yet still afraid
Lest aught in that palatial solitude
Lurked of most menace to a helpless maid.
Therefore forever faltering she stands,
Nor yet the last loose fold slips rippling from her hands.

Close by upon a beryl column, clad
In the fresh flower of adolescent grace,
They set the dear Bithynian shepherd lad,
The nude Antinous. That gentle face,
Forever beautiful, forever sad,
Shows but one aspect, moon-like, to our gaze,
Yet Fancy pictures how those lips could smile
At revelries in Rome, and banquets on the Nile.

And there were shapes of Beauty myriads more,

Clustering their rosy bridal bed around,
Whose scented breadth a silken fabric wore
Broidered with peacock hues on creamiest ground,
Fit to have graced the barge that Cydnus bore
Or Venus' bed in her enchanted mound,
While pillows swelled in stuffs of Orient dyes,
All broidered with strange fruits and birds of Paradise.

'Twas such a bower as Youth has visions of,
Thither with one fair spirit to retire,
Lie upon rose-leaves, sleep and wake with Love
And feast on kisses to the heart's desire;
Where by a casement opening on a grove,
Wide to the wood-winds and the sweet birds' choir,
A girl might stand and gaze into green boughs,
Like Credhe at the window of her golden house.

Or most like Vivien, the enchanting fay,
Where with her friend, in the strange tower they planned,
She lies and dreams eternity away,
Above the treetops in Broceliande,
Sometimes at twilight when the woods are gray
And wolf-packs howl far out across the lande,
Waking to love, while up behind the trees
The large midsummer moon lifts even so loved these.

For here, their pleasure was to come and sit
Oft when the sun sloped midway to the west,
Watching with sweet enjoyment interknit
The long light slant across the green earth's breast,
And clouds upon the ranges opposite,
Rolled up into a gleaming thundercrest,
Topple and break and fall in purple rain,
And mist of summer showers trail out across the plain.

Whereon the shafts of ardent light, far-flung
Across the luminous azure overhead,
Ofttimes in arcs of transient beauty hung
The fragmentary rainbow's green and red.
Joy it was here to love and to be young,
To watch the sun sink to his western bed,
And streaming back out of their flaming core
The vesperal aurora's glorious banners soar.

Tinging each altitude of heaven in turn,
Those fiery rays would sweep. The cumuli
That peeped above the mountain-tops would burn
Carmine a space; the cirrus-whorls on high,
More delicate than sprays of maiden fern,
Streak with pale rose the peacock-breasted sky,
Then blanch. As water-lilies fold at night,

Sank back into themselves those plumes of fervid light.

And they would watch the first faint stars appear,
The blue East blend with the blue hills below,
As lovers when their shuddering bliss draws near
Into one pulse of fluid rapture grow.
New fragrance on the freshening atmosphere
Would steal with evening, and the sunset glow
Draw deeper down into the wondrous west
Round vales of Proserpine and islands of the blest.

So dusk would come and mingle lake and shore,
The snow-peaks fade to frosty opaline,
To pearl the domed clouds the mountains bore,
Where late the sun's effulgent fire had been
Showing as darkness deepened more and more
The incandescent lightnings flare within,
And Night that furls the lily in the glen
And twines impatient arms would fall, and then, and then...

Sometimes the peasant, coming late from town
With empty panniers on his little drove
Past the old lookout when the Northern Crown
Glittered with Cygnus through the scented grove,
Would hear soft noise of lute-strings wafted down
And voices singing through the leaves above
Those songs that well from the warm heart that woos
At balconies in Merida or Vera Cruz.

And he would pause under the garden wall,
Caught in the spell of that voluptuous strain,
With all the sultry South in it, and all
Its importunity of love and pain;
And he would wait till the last passionate fall
Died on the night, and all was still again,
Then to his upland village wander home,
Marvelling whence that flood of elfin song might come.

O lyre that Love's white holy hands caress,
Youth, from thy bosom welled their passionate lays
Sweet opportunity for happiness
So brief, so passing beautiful - O days,
When to the heart's divine indulgences
All earth in smiling ministration pays
Thine was the source whose plenitude, past over,
What prize shall rest to pluck, what secret to discover!

The wake of color that follows her when May
Walks on the hills loose-haired and daisy-crowned,
The deep horizons of a summer's day,
Fair cities, and the pleasures that abound

Where music calls, and crowds in bright array
Gather by night to find and to be found;
What were these worth or all delightful things
Without thine eyes to read their true interpretings!

For thee the mountains open glorious gates,
To thee white arms put out from orient skies,
Earth, like a jewelled bride for one she waits,
Decks but to be delicious in thine eyes,
Thou guest of honor for one day, whose fetes
Eternity has travailed to devise;
Ah, grace them well in the brief hour they last!
Another's turn prepares, another follows fast.

Yet not without one fond memorial
Let my sun set who found the world so fair!
Frail verse, when Time the singer's coronal
Has rent, and stripped the rose-leaves from his hair,
Be thou my tablet on the temple wall!
Among the pious testimonials there,
Witness how sweetly on my heart as well
The miracles of dawn and starry evening fell!

Speak of one then who had the lust to feel,
And, from the hues that far horizons take,
And cloud and sunset, drank the wild appeal,
Too deep to live for aught but life's sweet sake,
Whose only motive was the will to kneel
Where Beauty's purest benediction spake,
Who only coveted what grove and field
And sunshine and green Earth and tender arms could yield

A nympholept, through pleasant days and drear
Seeking his faultless adolescent dream,
A pilgrim down the paths that disappear
In mist and rainbows on the world's extreme,
A helpless voyager who all too near
The mouth of Life's fair flower-bordered stream,
Clutched at Love's single respite in his need
More than the drowning swimmer clutches at a reed

That coming one whose feet in other days
Shall bleed like mine for ever having, more
Than any purpose, felt the need to praise
And seek the angelic image to adore,
In love with Love, its wonderful, sweet ways
Counting what most makes life worth living for,
That so some relic may be his to see
How I loved these things too and they were dear to me.

I sometimes think a conscious happiness

Mantles through all the rose's sentient vine
When summer winds with myriad calyces
Of bloom its clambering height incarnadine;
I sometimes think that cleaving lips, no less,
And limbs that crowned desires at length entwine
Are nerves through which that being drinks delight,
Whose frame is the green Earth robed round with day and night.

And such were theirs: the traveller without,
Pausing at night under the orchard trees,
Wondered and crossed himself in holy doubt,
For through their song and in the murmuring breeze
It seemed angelic choirs were all about
Mingling in universal harmonies,
As though, responsive to the chords they woke,
All Nature into sweet epithalamium broke.

And still they think a spirit haunts the place:
'Tis said, when Night has drawn her jewelled pall
And through the branches twinkling fireflies trace
Their mimic constellations, if it fall
That one should see the moon rise through the lace
Of blossomy boughs above the garden wall,
That surely would he take great ill thereof
And famish in a fit of unexpressive love.

But this I know not, for what time the wain
Was loosened and the lily's petal furled,
Then I would rise, climb the old wall again,
And pausing look forth on the sundown world,
Scan the wide reaches of the wondrous plain,
The hamlet sites where settling smoke lay curled,
The poplar-bordered roads, and far away
Fair snowpeaks colored with the sun's last ray.

Waves of faint sound would pulsate from afar
Faint song and preludes of the summer night;
Deep in the cloudless west the evening star
Hung 'twixt the orange and the emerald light;
From the dark vale where shades crepuscular
Dimmed the old grove-girt belfry glimmering white,
Throbbing, as gentlest breezes rose or fell,
Came the sweet invocation of the evening bell.

The Torture of Cuauhtemoc
Their strength had fed on this when Death's white arms
Came sleeved in vapors and miasmal dew,
Curling across the jungle's ferny floor,
Becking each fevered brain. On bleak divides,
Where Sleep grew niggardly for nipping cold

That twinged blue lips into a mouthed curse,
Not back to Seville and its sunny plains
Winged their brief-biding dreams, but once again,
Lords of a palace in Tenochtitlan,
They guarded Montezuma's treasure-hoard.
Gold, like some finny harvest of the sea,
Poured out knee deep around the rifted floors,
Shiny and sparkling, arms and crowns and rings:
Gold, sweet to toy with as beloved hair,
To plunge the lustful, crawling fingers down,
Arms elbow deep, and draw them out again,
And watch the glinting metal trickle off,
Even as at night some fisherman, home bound
With speckled cargo in his hollow keel
Caught off Campeche or the Isle of Pines,
Dips in his paddle, lifts it forth again,
And laughs to see the luminous white drops
Fall back in flakes of fire. . . . Gold was the dream
That cheered that desperate enterprise. And now?
Victory waited on the arms of Spain,
Fallen was the lovely city by the lake,
The sunny Venice of the western world;
There many corpses, rotting in the wind,
Poked up stiff limbs, but in the leprous rags
No jewel caught the sun, no tawny chain
Gleamed, as the prying halberds raked them o'er.
Pillage that ran red-handed through the streets
Came railing home at evening empty-palmed;
And they, on that sad night a twelvemonth gone,
Who, ounce by ounce, dear as their own life's blood
Retreating, cast the cumbrous load away:
They, when brown foemen lopped the bridges down,
Who tipped thonged chests into the stream below
And over wealth that might have ransomed kings
Passed on to safety; cheated, guerdonless
Found (through their fingers the bright booty slipped)
A city naked, of that golden dream
Shorn in one moment like a sunset sky.

Deep in a chamber that no cheerful ray
Purged of damp air, where in unbroken night
Black scorpions nested in the sooty beams,
Helpless and manacled they led him down
Cuauhtemotzin and other lords beside
All chieftains of the people, heroes all
And stripped their feathered robes and bound them there
On short stone settles sloping to the head,
But where the feet projected, underneath
Heaped the red coals. Their swarthy fronts illumed,
The bearded Spaniards, helmed and haubergeoned,
Paced up and down beneath the lurid vault.

Some kneeling fanned the glowing braziers; some
Stood at the sufferers' heads and all the while
Hissed in their ears: "The gold . . .the gold . . .the gold.
Where have ye hidden it - the chested gold?
Speak and the torments cease!"

They answered not.
Past those proud lips whose key their sovereign claimed
No accent fell to chide or to betray,
Only it chanced that bound beside the king
Lay one whom Nature, more than other men
Framing for delicate and perfumed ease,
Not yet, along the happy ways of Youth,
Had weaned from gentle usages so far
To teach that fortitude that warriors feel
And glory in the proof. He answered not,
But writhing with intolerable pain,
Convulsed in every limb, and all his face
Wrought to distortion with the agony,
Turned on his lord a look of wild appeal,
The secret half atremble on his lips,
Livid and quivering, that waited yet
For leave, for leave to utter it, one sign
One word, one little word, to ease his pain.

As one reclining in the banquet hall,
Propped on an elbow, garlanded with flowers,
Saw lust and greed and boisterous revelry
Surge round him on the tides of wine, but he,
Staunch in the ethic of an antique school
Stoic or Cynic or of Pyrrho's mind
With steady eyes surveyed the unbridled scene,
Himself impassive, silent, self-contained:
So sat the Indian prince, with brow unblanched,
Amid the tortured and the torturers.
He who had seen his hopes made desolate,
His realm despoiled, his early crown deprived him,
And watched while Pestilence and Famine piled
His stricken people in their reeking doors,
Whence glassy eyes looked out and lean brown arms
Stretched up to greet him in one last farewell
As back and forth he paced along the streets
With words of hopeless comfort, what was this
That one should weaken now? He weakened not.
Whate'er was in his heart, he neither dealt
In pity nor in scorn, but, turning round,
Met that racked visage with his own unmoved,
Bent on the sufferer his mild calm eyes,
And while the pangs smote sharper, in a voice,
As who would speak not all in gentleness
Nor all disdain, said: "Yes! And am -I- then

Upon a bed of roses?"

Stung with shame
Shame bitterer than his anguish to betray
Such cowardice before the man he loved,
And merit such rebuke, the boy grew calm;
And stilled his struggling limbs and moaning cries,
And shook away his tears, and strove to smile,
And turned his face against the wall and died.

The Nympholept
There was a boy, not above childish fears
With steps that faltered now and straining ears,
Timid, irresolute, yet dauntless still,
Who one bright dawn, when each remotest hill
Stood sharp and clear in Heaven's unclouded blue
And all Earth shimmered with fresh-beaded dew,
Risen in the first beams of the gladdening sun,
Walked up into the mountains. One by one
Each towering trunk beneath his sturdy stride
Fell back, and ever wider and more wide
The boundless prospect opened. Long he strayed,
From dawn till the last trace of slanting shade
Had vanished from the canyons, and, dismayed
At that far length to which his path had led,
He paused at such a height where overhead
The clouds hung close, the air came thin and chill,
And all was hushed and calm and very still,
Save, from abysmal gorges, where the sound
Of tumbling waters rose, and all around
The pines, by those keen upper currents blown,
Muttered in multitudinous monotone.
Here, with the wind in lovely locks laid bare,
With arms oft raised in dedicative prayer,
Lost in mute rapture and adoring wonder,
He stood, till the far noise of noontide thunder,
Rolled down upon the muffled harmonies
Of wind and waterfall and whispering trees,
Made loneliness more lone. Some Panic fear
Would seize him then, as they who seemed to hear
In Tracian valleys or Thessalian woods
The god's hallooing wake the leafy solitudes;
I think it was the same: some piercing sense
Of Deity's pervasive immanence,
The Life that visible Nature doth indwell
Grown great and near and all but palpable. . .
He might not linger, but with winged strides
Like one pursued, fled down the mountain-sides
Down the long ridge that edged the steep ravine,
By glade and flowery lawn and upland green,

And never paused nor felt assured again
But where the grassy foothills opened. Then,
While shadows lengthened on the plain below
And the sun vanished and the sunset-glow
Looked back upon the world with fervid eye
Through the barred windows of the western sky,
Homeward he fared, while many a look behind
Showed the receding ranges dim-outlined,
Highland and hollow where his path had lain,
Veiled in deep purple of the mountain rain.

The Wanderer
To see the clouds his spirit yearned toward so
Over new mountains piled and unploughed waves,
Back of old-storied spires and architraves
To watch Arcturus rise or Fomalhaut,

And roused by street-cries in strange tongues when day
Flooded with gold some domed metropolis,
Between new towers to waken and new bliss
Spread on his pillow in a wondrous way:

These were his joys. Oft under bulging crates,
Coming to market with his morning load,
The peasant found him early on his road
To greet the sunrise at the city-gates,

There where the meadows waken in its rays,
Golden with mist, and the great roads commence,
And backward, where the chimney-tops are dense,
Cathedral-arches glimmer through the haze.

White dunes that breaking show a strip of sea,
A plowman and his team against the blue,
Swiss pastures musical with cowbells, too,
And poplar-lined canals in Picardie,

And coast-towns where the vultures back and forth
Sail in the clear depths of the tropic sky,
And swallows in the sunset where they fly
Over gray Gothic cities in the north,

And the wine-cellar and the chorus there,
The dance-hall and a face among the crowd,
Were all delights that made him sing aloud
For joy to sojourn in a world so fair.

Back of his footsteps as he journeyed fell
Range after range; ahead blue hills emerged.
Before him tireless to applaud it surged

The sweet interminable spectacle.

And like the west behind a sundown sea
Shone the past joys his memory retraced,
And bright as the blue east he always faced
Beckoned the loves and joys that were to be.

From every branch a blossom for his brow
He gathered, singing down Life's flower-lined road,
And youth impelled his spirit as he strode
Like winged Victory on the galley's prow.

That Loveliness whose being sun and star,
Green Earth and dawn and amber evening robe,
That lamp whereof the opalescent globe
The season's emulative splendors are,

That veiled divinity whose beams transpire
From every pore of universal space,
As the fair soul illumes the lovely face
That was his guest, his passion, his desire.

His heart the love of Beauty held as hides
One gem most pure a casket of pure gold.
It was too rich a lesser thing to hold;
It was not large enough for aught besides.

The Need to Love
The need to love that all the stars obey
Entered my heart and banished all beside.
Bare were the gardens where I used to stray;
Faded the flowers that one time satisfied.

Before the beauty of the west on fire,
The moonlit hills from cloister-casements viewed,
Cloud-like arose the image of desire,
And cast out peace and maddened solitude.

I sought the City and the hopes it held:
With smoke and brooding vapors intercurled,
As the thick roofs and walls close-paralleled
Shut out the fair horizons of the world

A truant from the fields and rustic joy,
In my changed thought that image even so
Shut out the gods I worshipped as a boy
And all the pure delights I used to know.

Often the veil has trembled at some tide
Of lovely reminiscence and revealed

How much of beauty Nature holds beside
Sweet lips that sacrifice and arms that yield:

Clouds, window-framed, beyond the huddled eaves
When summer cumulates their golden chains,
Or from the parks the smell of burning leaves,
Fragrant of childhood in the country lanes,

An organ-grinder's melancholy tune
In rainy streets, or from an attic sill
The blue skies of a windy afternoon
Where our kites climbed once from some grassy hill:

And my soul once more would be wrapped entire
In the pure peace and blessing of those years
Before the fierce infection of Desire
Had ravaged all the flesh. Through starting tears

Shone that lost Paradise; but, if it did,
Again ere long the prison-shades would fall
That Youth condemns itself to walk amid,
So narrow, but so beautiful withal.

And I have followed Fame with less devotion,
And kept no real ambition but to see
Rise from the foam of Nature's sunlit ocean
My dream of palpable divinity;

And aught the world contends for to mine eye
Seemed not so real a meaning of success
As only once to clasp before I die
My vision of embodied happiness.

El Extraviado
Over the radiant ridges borne out on the offshore wind,
I have sailed as a butterfly sails whose priming wings unfurled
Leave the familiar gardens and visited fields behind
To follow a cloud in the east rose-flushed on the rim of the world.

I have strayed from the trodden highway for walking with upturned eyes
On the way of the wind in the treetops, and the drift of the tinted rack.
For the will to be losing no wonder of sunny or starlit skies
I have chosen the sod for my pillow and a threadbare coat for my back.

Evening of ample horizons, opaline, delicate, pure,
Shadow of clouds on green valleys, trailed over meadows and trees,
Cities of ardent adventure where the harvests of Joy mature,
Forests whose murmuring voices are amorous prophecies,

World of romance and profusion, still round my journey spread

The glamours, the glints, the enthralments, the nurture of one whose feet
From hours unblessed by beauty nor lighted by love have fled
As the shade of the tomb on his pathway and the scent of the winding-sheet.

I never could rest from roving nor put from my heart this need
To be seeing how lovably Nature in flower and face hath wrought,
In flower and meadow and mountain and heaven where the white clouds breed
And the cunning of silken meshes where the heart's desire lies caught.

Over the azure expanses, on the offshore breezes borne,
I have sailed as a butterfly sails, nor recked where the impulse led,
Sufficed with the sunshine and freedom, the warmth and the summer morn,
The infinite glory surrounding, the infinite blue ahead.

La Nue
Oft when sweet music undulated round,
Like the full moon out of a perfumed sea
Thine image from the waves of blissful sound
Rose and thy sudden light illumined me.

And in the country, leaf and flower and air
Would alter and the eternal shape emerge;
Because they spoke of thee the fields seemed fair,
And Joy to wait at the horizon's verge.

The little cloud-gaps in the east that filled
Gray afternoons with bits of tenderest blue
Were windows in a palace pearly-silled
That thy voluptuous traits came glimmering through.

And in the city, dominant desire
For which men toil within its prison-bars,
I watched thy white feet moving in the mire
And thy white forehead hid among the stars.

Mystical, feminine, provoking, nude,
Radiant there with rosy arms outspread,
Sum of fulfillment, sovereign attitude,
Sensual with laughing lips and thrown-back head,

Draped in the rainbow on the summer hills,
Hidden in sea-mist down the hot coast-line,
Couched on the clouds that fiery sunset fills,
Blessed, remote, impersonal, divine;

The gold all color and grace are folded o'er,
The warmth all beauty and tenderness embower,
Thou quiverest at Nature's perfumed core,
The pistil of a myriad-petalled flower.

Round thee revolves, illimitably wide,
The world's desire, as stars around their pole.
Round thee all earthly loveliness beside
Is but the radiate, infinite aureole.

Thou art the poem on the cosmic page
In rubric written on its golden ground
That Nature paints her flowers and foliage
And rich-illumined commentary round.

Thou art the rose that the world's smiles and tears
Hover about like butterflies and bees.
Thou art the theme the music of the spheres
Echoes in endless, variant harmonies.

Thou art the idol in the altar-niche
Faced by Love's congregated worshippers,
Thou art the holy sacrament round which
The vast cathedral is the universe.

Thou art the secret in the crystal where,
For the last light upon the mystery Man,
In his lone tower and ultimate despair,
Searched the gray-bearded Zoroastrian.

And soft and warm as in the magic sphere,
Deep-orbed as in its erubescent fire,
So in my heart thine image would appear,
Curled round with the red flames of my desire.

All That's Not Love . . .
All that's not love is the dearth of my days,
The leaves of the volume with rubric unwrit,
The temple in times without prayer, without praise,
The altar unset and the candle unlit.

Let me survive not the lovable sway
Of early desire, nor see when it goes
The courts of Life's abbey in ivied decay,
Whence sometime sweet anthems and incense arose.

The delicate hues of its sevenfold rings
The rainbow outlives not; their yellow and blue
The butterfly sees not dissolve from his wings,
But even with their beauty life fades from them too.

No more would I linger past Love's ardent bounds
Nor live for aught else but the joy that it craves,
That, burden and essence of all that surrounds,
Is the song in the wind and the smile on the waves.

Paris

I

First, London, for its myriads; for its height,
Manhattan heaped in towering stalagmite;
But Paris for the smoothness of the paths
That lead the heart unto the heart's delight. . . .

Fair loiterer on the threshold of those days
When there's no lovelier prize the world displays
Than, having beauty and your twenty years,
You have the means to conquer and the ways,

And coming where the crossroads separate
And down each vista glories and wonders wait,
Crowning each path with pinnacles so fair
You know not which to choose, and hesitate

Oh, go to Paris. . . . In the midday gloom
Of some old quarter take a little room
That looks off over Paris and its towers
From Saint Gervais round to the Emperor's Tomb,

So high that you can hear a mating dove
Croon down the chimney from the roof above,
See Notre Dame and know how sweet it is
To wake between Our Lady and our love.

And have a little balcony to bring
Fair plants to fill with verdure and blossoming,
That sparrows seek, to feed from pretty hands,
And swallows circle over in the Spring.

There of an evening you shall sit at ease
In the sweet month of flowering chestnut-trees,
There with your little darling in your arms,
Your pretty dark-eyed Manon or Louise.

And looking out over the domes and towers
That chime the fleeting quarters and the hours,
While the bright clouds banked eastward back of them
Blush in the sunset, pink as hawthorn flowers,

You cannot fail to think, as I have done,
Some of life's ends attained, so you be one
Who measures life's attainment by the hours
That Joy has rescued from oblivion.

II

Come out into the evening streets. The green light lessens in the west.

The city laughs and liveliest her fervid pulse of pleasure beats.

The belfry on Saint Severin strikes eight across the smoking eaves:
Come out under the lights and leaves
to the Reine Blanche on Saint Germain. . . .

Now crowded diners fill the floor of brasserie and restaurant.
Shrill voices cry "L'Intransigeant," and corners echo "Paris-Sport."

Where rows of tables from the street are screened with shoots of box and bay,
The ragged minstrels sing and play and gather sous from those that eat.

And old men stand with menu-cards, inviting passers-by to dine
On the bright terraces that line the Latin Quarter boulevards. . . .

But, having drunk and eaten well, 'tis pleasant then to stroll along
And mingle with the merry throng that promenades on Saint Michel.

Here saunter types of every sort. The shoddy jostle with the chic:
Turk and Roumanian and Greek; student and officer and sport;

Slavs with their peasant, Christ-like heads, and courtezans like powdered moths,
And peddlers from Algiers, with cloths bright-hued and stitched with golden threads;

And painters with big, serious eyes go rapt in dreams, fantastic shapes
In corduroys and Spanish capes and locks uncut and flowing ties;

And lovers wander two by two, oblivious among the press,
And making one of them no less, all lovers shall be dear to you:

All laughing lips you move among, all happy hearts that, knowing what
Makes life worth while, have wasted not the sweet reprieve of being young.

"Comment ca va!" "Mon vieux!" "Mon cher!" Friends greet and banter as they pass.
'Tis sweet to see among the mass comrades and lovers everywhere,

A law that's sane, a Love that's free, and men of every birth and blood
Allied in one great brotherhood of Art and Joy and Poverty. . . .

The open cafe-windows frame loungers at their liqueurs and beer,
And walking past them one can hear fragments of Tosca and Boheme.

And in the brilliant-lighted door of cinemas the barker calls,
And lurid posters paint the walls with scenes of Love and crime and war.

But follow past the flaming lights, borne onward with the stream of feet,
Where Bullier's further up the street is marvellous on Thursday nights.

Here all Bohemia flocks apace; you could not often find elsewhere
So many happy heads and fair assembled in one time and place.

Under the glare and noise and heat the galaxy of dancing whirls,
Smokers, with covered heads, and girls dressed in the costume of the street.

From tables packed around the wall the crowds that drink and frolic there
Spin serpentines into the air far out over the reeking hall,

That, settling where the coils unroll, tangle with pink and green and blue
The crowds that rag to "Hitchy-koo" and boston to the "Barcarole". . . .

Here Mimi ventures, at fifteen, to make her debut in romance,
And join her sisters in the dance and see the life that they have seen.

Her hair, a tight hat just allows to brush beneath the narrow brim,
Docked, in the model's present whim, 'frise' and banged above the brows.

Uncorseted, her clinging dress with every step and turn betrays,
In pretty and provoking ways her adolescent loveliness,

As guiding Gaby or Lucile she dances, emulating them
In each disturbing stratagem and each lascivious appeal.

Each turn a challenge, every pose an invitation to compete,
Along the maze of whirling feet the grave-eyed little wanton goes,

And, flaunting all the hue that lies in childish cheeks and nubile waist,
She passes, charmingly unchaste, illumining ignoble eyes. . . .

But now the blood from every heart leaps madder through abounding veins
As first the fascinating strains of "El Irresistible" start.

Caught in the spell of pulsing sound, impatient elbows lift and yield
The scented softnesses they shield to arms that catch and close them round,

Surrender, swift to be possessed, the silken supple forms beneath
To all the bliss the measures breathe and all the madness they suggest.

Crowds congregate and make a ring. Four deep they stand and strain to see
The tango in its ecstasy of glowing lives that clasp and cling.

Lithe limbs relaxed, exalted eyes fastened on vacancy, they seem
To float upon the perfumed stream of some voluptuous Paradise,

Or, rapt in some Arabian Night, to rock there, cradled and subdued,
In a luxurious lassitude of rhythm and sensual delight.

And only when the measures cease and terminate the flowing dance
They waken from their magic trance and join the cries that clamor "Bis!" . . .

Midnight adjourns the festival. The couples climb the crowded stair,
And out into the warm night air go singing fragments of the ball.

Close-folded in desire they pass, or stop to drink and talk awhile
In the cafes along the mile from Bullier's back to Montparnasse:

The "Closerie" or "La Rotonde", where smoking, under lamplit trees,
Sit Art's enamored devotees, chatting across their 'brune' and 'blonde'. . . .

Make one of them and come to know sweet Paris, not as many do,
Seeing but the folly of the few, the froth, the tinsel, and the show

But taking some white proffered hand that from Earth's barren every day
Can lead you by the shortest way into Love's florid fairyland.

And that divine enchanted life that lurks under Life's common guise
That city of romance that lies within the City's toil and strife

Shall, knocking, open to your hands, for Love is all its golden key,
And one's name murmured tenderly the only magic it demands.

And when all else is gray and void in the vast gulf of memory,
Green islands of delight shall be all blessed moments so enjoyed:

When vaulted with the city skies, on its cathedral floors you stood,
And, priest of a bright brotherhood, performed the mystic sacrifice,

At Love's high altar fit to stand, with fire and incense aureoled,
The celebrant in cloth of gold with Spring and Youth on either hand.

III
Choral Song
Have ye gazed on its grandeur
Or stood where it stands
With opal and amber
Adorning the lands,
And orcharded domes
Of the hue of all flowers?
Sweet melody roams
Through its blossoming bowers,
Sweet bells usher in from its belfries the train of the honey-sweet hour.

A city resplendent,
Fulfilled of good things,
On its ramparts are pendent
The bucklers of kings.
Broad banners unfurled
Are afloat in its air.
The lords of the world
Look for harborage there.
None finds save he comes as a bridegroom, having roses and vine in his hair.

'Tis the city of Lovers,
There many paths meet.

Blessed he above others,
With faltering feet,
Who past its proud spires
Intends not nor hears
The noise of its lyres
Grow faint in his ears!
Men reach it through portals of triumph, but leave through a postern of tears.

It was thither, ambitious,
We came for Youth's right,
When our lips yearned for kisses
As moths for the light,
When our souls cried for Love
As for life-giving rain
Wan leaves of the grove,
Withered grass of the plain,
And our flesh ached for Love-flesh beside it with bitter, intolerable pain.

Under arbor and trellis,
Full of flutes, full of flowers,
What mad fortunes befell us,
What glad orgies were ours!
In the days of our youth,
In our festal attire,
When the sweet flesh was smooth,
When the swift blood was fire,
And all Earth paid in orange and purple to pavilion the bed of Desire!

The Sultan's Palace
My spirit only lived to look on Beauty's face,
As only when they clasp the arms seem served aright;
As in their flesh inheres the impulse to embrace,
To gaze on Loveliness was my soul's appetite.

I have roamed far in search; white road and plunging bow
Were keys in the blue doors where my desire was set;
Obedient to their lure, my lips and laughing brow
The hill-showers and the spray of many seas have wet.

Hot are enamored hands, the fragrant zone unbound,
To leave no dear delight unfelt, unfondled o'er,
The will possessed my heart to girdle Earth around
With their insatiate need to wonder and adore.

The flowers in the fields, the surf upon the sands,
The sunset and the clouds it turned to blood and wine,
Were shreds of the thin veil behind whose beaded strands
A radiant visage rose, serene, august, divine.

A noise of summer wind astir in starlit trees,

A song where sensual love's delirium rose and fell,
Were rites that moved my soul more than the devotee's
When from the blazing choir rings out the altar bell.

I woke amid the pomp of a proud palace; writ
In tinted arabesque on walls that gems o'erlay,
The names of caliphs were who once held court in it,
Their baths and bowers were mine to dwell in for a day.

Their robes and rings were mine to draw from shimmering trays
Brocades and broidered silks, topaz and tourmaline
Their turban-cloths to wind in proud capricious ways,
And fasten plumes and pearls and pendent sapphires in.

I rose; far music drew my steps in fond pursuit
Down tessellated floors and towering peristyles:
Through groves of colonnades fair lamps were blushing fruit,
On seas of green mosaic soft rugs were flowery isles.

And there were verdurous courts that scalloped arches wreathed,
Where fountains plashed in bowls of lapis lazuli.
Through enigmatic doors voluptuous accents breathed,
And having Youth I had their Open Sesame.

I paused where shadowy walls were hung with cloths of gold,
And tinted twilight streamed through storied panes above.
In lamplit alcoves deep as flowers when they unfold
Soft cushions called to rest and fragrant fumes to love.

I hungered; at my hand delicious dainties teemed
Fair pyramids of fruit; pastry in sugared piles.
I thirsted; in cool cups inviting vintage beamed
Sweet syrups from the South; brown muscat from the isles.

I yearned for passionate Love; faint gauzes fell away.
Pillowed in rosy light I found my heart's desire.
Over the silks and down her florid beauty lay,
As over orient clouds the sunset's coral fire.

Joys that had smiled afar, a visionary form,
Behind the ranges hid, remote and rainbow-dyed,
Drew near unto my heart, a wonder soft and warm,
To touch, to stroke, to clasp, to sleep and wake beside.

Joy, that where summer seas and hot horizons shone
Had been the outspread arms I gave my youth to seek,
Drew near; awhile its pulse strove sweetly with my own,
Awhile I felt its breath astir upon my cheek.

I was so happy there; so fleeting was my stay,
What wonder if, assailed with vistas so divine,

I only lived to search and sample them the day
When between dawn and dusk the sultan's courts were mine!

Speak not of other worlds of happiness to be,
As though in any fond imaginary sphere
Lay more to tempt man's soul to immortality
Than ripens for his bliss abundant now and here!

Flowerlike I hope to die as flowerlike was my birth.
Rooted in Nature's just benignant law like them,
I want no better joys than those that from green Earth
My spirit's blossom drew through the sweet body's stem.

I see no dread in death, no horror to abhor.
I never thought it else than but to cease to dwell
Spectator, and resolve most naturally once more
Into the dearly loved eternal spectacle.

Unto the fields and flowers this flesh I found so fair
I yield; do you, dear friend, over your rose-crowned wine,
Murmur my name some day as though my lips were there,
And frame your mouth as though its blushing kiss were mine.

Yea, where the banquet-hall is brilliant with young men,
You whose bright youth it might have thrilled my breast to know,
Drink . . . and perhaps my lips, insatiate even then
Of lips to hang upon, may find their loved ones so.

Unto the flush of dawn and evening I commend
This immaterial self and flamelike part of me,
Unto the azure haze that hangs at the world's end,
The sunshine on the hills, the starlight on the sea,

Unto angelic Earth, whereof the lives of those
Who love and dream great dreams and deeply feel may be
The elemental cells and nervules that compose
Its divine consciousness and joy and harmony.

Fragments
I
In that fair capital where Pleasure, crowned
Amidst her myriad courtiers, riots and rules,
I too have been a suitor. Radiant eyes
Were my life's warmth and sunshine, outspread arms
My gilded deep horizons. I rejoiced
In yielding to all amorous influence
And multiple impulsion of the flesh,
To feel within my being surge and sway
The force that all the stars acknowledge too.
Amid the nebulous humanity

Where I an atom crawled and cleaved and sundered,
I saw a million motions, but one law;
And from the city's splendor to my eyes
The vapors passed and there was nought but Love,
A ferment turbulent, intensely fair,
Where Beauty beckoned and where Strength pursued.

II
There was a time when I thought much of Fame,
And laid the golden edifice to be
That in the clear light of eternity
Should fitly house the glory of my name.

But swifter than my fingers pushed their plan,
Over the fair foundation scarce begun,
While I with lovers dallied in the sun,
The ivy clambered and the rose-vine ran.

And now, too late to see my vision, rise,
In place of golden pinnacles and towers,
Only some sunny mounds of leaves and flowers,
Only beloved of birds and butterflies.

My friends were duped, my favorers deceived;
But sometimes, musing sorrowfully there,
That flowered wreck has seemed to me so fair
I scarce regret the temple unachieved.

III
For there were nights . . . my love to him whose brow
Has glistened with the spoils of nights like those,
Home turning as a conqueror turns home,
What time green dawn down every street uprears
Arches of triumph! He has drained as well
Joy's perfumed bowl and cried as I have cried:
Be Fame their mistress whom Love passes by.
This only matters: from some flowery bed,
Laden with sweetness like a homing bee,
If one have known what bliss it is to come,
Bearing on hands and breast and laughing lips
The fragrance of his youth's dear rose. To him
The hills have bared their treasure, the far clouds
Unveiled the vision that o'er summer seas
Drew on his thirsting arms. This last thing known,
He can court danger, laugh at perilous odds,
And, pillowed on a memory so sweet,
Unto oblivious eternity
Without regret yield his victorious soul,
The blessed pilgrim of a vow fulfilled.

IV

What is Success? Out of the endless ore
Of deep desire to coin the utmost gold
Of passionate memory; to have lived so well
That the fifth moon, when it swims up once more
Through orchard boughs where mating orioles build
And apple flowers unfold,
Find not of that dear need that all things tell
The heart unburdened nor the arms unfilled.

O Love, whereof my boyhood was the dream,
My youth the beautiful novitiate,
Life was so slight a thing and thou so great,
How could I make thee less than all-supreme!
In thy sweet transports not alone I thought
Mingled the twain that panted breast to breast.
The sun and stars throbbed with them; they were caught
Into the pulse of Nature and possessed
By the same light that consecrates it so.
Love! 'tis the payment of the debt we owe
The beauty of the world, and whensoe'er
In silks and perfume and unloosened hair
The loveliness of lovers, face to face,
Lies folded in the adorable embrace,
Doubt not as of a perfect sacrifice
That soul partakes whose inspiration fills
The springtime and the depth of summer skies,
The rainbow and the clouds behind the hills,
That excellence in earth and air and sea
That makes things as they are the real divinity.

Thirty Sonnets:

Sonnet I
Down the strait vistas where a city street
Fades in pale dust and vaporous distances,
Stained with far fumes the light grows less and less
And the sky reddens round the day's retreat.
Now out of orient chambers, cool and sweet,
Like Nature's pure lustration, Dusk comes down.
Now the lamps brighten and the quickening town
Rings with the trample of returning feet.
And Pleasure, risen from her own warm mould
Sunk all the drowsy and unloved daylight
In layers of odorous softness, Paphian girls
Cover with gauze, with satin, and with pearls,
Crown, and about her spangly vestments fold
The ermine of the empire of the Night.

Sonnet II

Her courts are by the flux of flaming ways,
Between the rivers and the illumined sky
Whose fervid depths reverberate from on high
Fierce lustres mingled in a fiery haze.
They mark it inland; blithe and fair of face
Her suitors follow, guessing by the glare
Beyond the hilltops in the evening air
How bright the cressets at her portals blaze.
On the pure fronts Defeat ere many a day
Falls like the soot and dirt on city-snow;
There hopes deferred lie sunk in piteous seams.
Her paths are disillusion and decay,
With ruins piled and unapparent woe,
The graves of Beauty and the wreck of dreams.

Sonnet III
There was a youth around whose early way
White angels hung in converse and sweet choir,
Teaching in summer clouds his thought to stray,
In cloud and far horizon to desire.
His life was nursed in beauty, like the stream
Born of clear showers and the mountain dew,
Close under snow-clad summits where they gleam
Forever pure against heaven's orient blue.
Within the city's shades he walked at last.
Faint and more faint in sad recessional
Down the dim corridors of Time outworn,
A chorus ebbed from that forsaken past,
A hymn of glories fled beyond recall
With the lost heights and splendor of life's morn.

Sonnet IV
Up at his attic sill the South wind came
And days of sun and storm but never peace.
Along the town's tumultuous arteries
He heard the heart-throbs of a sentient frame:
Each night the whistles in the bay, the same
Whirl of incessant wheels and clanging cars:
For smoke that half obscured, the circling stars
Burnt like his youth with but a sickly flame.
Up to his attic came the city cries
The throes with which her iron sinews heave
And yet forever behind prison doors
Welled in his heart and trembled in his eyes
The light that hangs on desert hills at eve
And tints the sea on solitary shores. . . .

Sonnet V

A tide of beauty with returning May
Floods the fair city; from warm pavements fume
Odors endeared; down avenues in bloom
The chestnut-trees with phallic spires are gay.
Over the terrace flows the thronged cafe;
The boulevards are streams of hurrying sound;
And through the streets, like veins when they abound,
The lust for pleasure throbs itself away.
Here let me live, here let me still pursue
Phantoms of bliss that beckon and recede,
Thy strange allurements, City that I love,
Maze of romance, where I have followed too
The dream Youth treasures of its dearest need
And stars beyond thy towers bring tidings of.

Sonnet VI
Give me the treble of thy horns and hoofs,
The ponderous undertones of 'bus and tram,
A garret and a glimpse across the roofs
Of clouds blown eastward over Notre Dame,
The glad-eyed streets and radiant gatherings
Where I drank deep the bliss of being young,
The strife and sweet potential flux of things
I sought Youth's dream of happiness among!
It walks here aureoled with the city-light,
Forever through the myriad-featured mass
Flaunting not far its fugitive embrace,
Heard sometimes in a song across the night,
Caught in a perfume from the crowds that pass,
And when love yields to love seen face to face.

Sonnet VII
To me, a pilgrim on that journey bound
Whose stations Beauty's bright examples are,
As of a silken city famed afar
Over the sands for wealth and holy ground,
Came the report of one, a woman crowned
With all perfection, blemishless and high,
As the full moon amid the moonlit sky,
With the world's praise and wonder clad around.
And I who held this notion of success:
To leave no form of Nature's loveliness
Unworshipped, if glad eyes have access there,
Beyond all earthly bounds have made my goal
To find where that sweet shrine is and extol
The hand that triumphed in a work so fair.

Sonnet VIII

Oft as by chance, a little while apart
The pall of empty, loveless hours withdrawn,
Sweet Beauty, opening on the impoverished heart,
Beams like the jewel on the breast of dawn:
Not though high heaven should rend would deeper awe
Fill me than penetrates my spirit thus,
Nor all those signs the Patmian prophet saw
Seem a new heaven and earth so marvelous;
But, clad thenceforth in iridescent dyes,
The fair world glistens, and in after days
The memory of kind lips and laughing eyes
Lives in my step and lightens all my face,
So they who found the Earthly Paradise
Still breathed, returned, of that sweet, joyful place.

Sonnet IX
Amid the florid multitude her face
Was like the full moon seen behind the lace
Of orchard boughs where clouded blossoms part
When Spring shines in the world and in the heart.
As the full-moon-beams to the ferny floor
Of summer woods through flower and foliage pour,
So to my being's innermost recess
Flooded the light of so much loveliness;
She held as in a vase of priceless ware
The wine that over arid ways and bare
My youth was the pathetic thirsting for,
And where she moved the veil of Nature grew
Diaphanous and that radiance mantled through
Which, when I see, I tremble and adore.

Sonnet X
A splendor, flamelike, born to be pursued,
With palms extent for amorous charity
And eyes incensed with love for all they see,
A wonder more to be adored than wooed,
On whom the grace of conscious womanhood
Adorning every little thing she does
Sits like enchantment, making glorious
A careless pose, a casual attitude;
Around her lovely shoulders mantle-wise
Hath come the realm of those old fabulous queens
Whose storied loves are Art's rich heritage,
To keep alive in this our latter age
That force that moving through sweet Beauty's means
Lifts up Man's soul to towering enterprise.

Sonnet XI

When among creatures fair of countenance
Love comes enformed in such proud character,
So far as other beauty yields to her,
So far the breast with fiercer longing pants;
I bless the spot, and hour, and circumstance,
That wed desire to a thing so high,
And say, Glad soul, rejoice, for thou and I
Of bliss unpaired are made participants;
Hence have come ardent thoughts and waking dreams
That, feeding Fancy from so sweet a cup,
Leave it no lust for gross imaginings.
Through her the woman's perfect beauty gleams
That while it gazes lifts the spirit up
To that high source from which all beauty springs.

Sonnet XII
Like as a dryad, from her native bole
Coming at dusk, when the dim stars emerge,
To a slow river at whose silent verge
Tall poplars tremble and deep grasses roll,
Come thou no less and, kneeling in a shoal
Of the freaked flag and meadow buttercup,
Bend till thine image from the pool beam up
Arched with blue heaven like an aureole.
See how adorable in fancy then
Lives the fair face it mirrors even so,
O thou whose beauty moving among men
Is like the wind's way on the woods below,
Filling all nature where its pathway lies
With arms that supplicate and trembling sighs.

Sonnet XIII
I fancied, while you stood conversing there,
Superb, in every attitude a queen,
Her ermine thus Boadicea bare,
So moved amid the multitude Faustine.
My life, whose whole religion Beauty is,
Be charged with sin if ever before yours
A lesser feeling crossed my mind than his
Who owning grandeur marvels and adores.
Nay, rather in my dream-world's ivory tower
I made your image the high pearly sill,
And mounting there in many a wistful hour,
Burdened with love, I trembled and was still,
Seeing discovered from that azure height
Remote, untrod horizons of delight.

Sonnet XIV

It may be for the world of weeds and tares
And dearth in Nature of sweet Beauty's rose
That oft as Fortune from ten thousand shows
One from the train of Love's true courtiers
Straightway on him who gazes, unawares,
Deep wonder seizes and swift trembling grows,
Reft by that sight of purpose and repose,
Hardly its weight his fainting breast upbears.
Then on the soul from some ancestral place
Floods back remembrance of its heavenly birth,
When, in the light of that serener sphere,
It saw ideal beauty face to face
That through the forms of this our meaner Earth
Shines with a beam less steadfast and less clear.

Sonnet XV
Above the ruin of God's holy place,
Where man-forsaken lay the bleeding rood,
Whose hands, when men had craved substantial food,
Gave not, nor folded when they cried, Embrace,
I saw exalted in the latter days
Her whom west winds with natal foam bedewed,
Wafted toward Cyprus, lily-breasted, nude,
Standing with arms out-stretched and flower-like face.
And, sick with all those centuries of tears
Shed in the penance for factitious woe,
Once more I saw the nations at her feet,
For Love shone in their eyes, and in their ears
Come unto me, Love beckoned them, for lo!
The breast your lips abjured is still as sweet.

Sonnet XVI
Who shall invoke her, who shall be her priest,
With single rites the common debt to pay?
On some green headland fronting to the East
Our fairest boy shall kneel at break of day.
Naked, uplifting in a laden tray
New milk and honey and sweet-tinctured wine,
Not without twigs of clustering apple-spray
To wreath a garland for Our Lady's shrine.
The morning planet poised above the sea
Shall drop sweet influence through her drowsing lid;
Dew-drenched, his delicate virginity
Shall scarce disturb the flowers he kneels amid,
That, waked so lightly, shall lift up their eyes,
Cushion his knees, and nod between his thighs.

Kyrenaikos

Lay me where soft Cyrene rambles down
In grove and garden to the sapphire sea;
Twine yellow roses for the drinker's crown;
Let music reach and fair heads circle me,
Watching blue ocean where the white sails steer
Fruit-laden forth or with the wares and news
Of merchant cities seek our harbors here,
Careless how Corinth fares, how Syracuse;
But here, with love and sleep in her caress,
Warm night shall sink and utterly persuade
The gentle doctrine Aristippus bare,
Night-winds, and one whose white youth's loveliness,
In a flowered balcony beside me laid,
Dreams, with the starlight on her fragrant hair.

Antinous
Stretched on a sunny bank he lay at rest,
Ferns at his elbow, lilies round his knees,
With sweet flesh patterned where the cool turf pressed,
Flowerlike crept o'er with emerald aphides.
Single he couched there, to his circling flocks
Piping at times some happy shepherd's tune,
Nude, with the warm wind in his golden locks,
And arched with the blue Asian afternoon.
Past him, gorse-purpled, to the distant coast
Rolled the clear foothills. There his white-walled town,
There, a blue band, the placid Euxine lay.
Beyond, on fields of azure light embossed
He watched from noon till dewy eve came down
The summer clouds pile up and fade away.

Vivien
Her eyes under their lashes were blue pools
Fringed round with lilies; her bright hair unfurled
Clothed her as sunshine clothes the summer world.
Her robes were gauzes, gold and green and gules,
All furry things flocked round her, from her hand
Nibbling their foods and fawning at her feet.
Two peacocks watched her where she made her seat
Beside a fountain in Broceliande.
Sometimes she sang. . . . Whoever heard forgot
Errand and aim, and knights at noontide here,
Riding from fabulous gestes beyond the seas,
Would follow, tranced, and seek . . .and find her not . . .
But wake that night, lost, by some woodland mere,
Powdered with stars and rimmed with silent trees.

I Loved . . .

I loved illustrious cities and the crowds
That eddy through their incandescent nights.
I loved remote horizons with far clouds
Girdled, and fringed about with snowy heights.
I loved fair women, their sweet, conscious ways
Of wearing among hands that covet and plead
The rose ablossom at the rainbow's base
That bounds the world's desire and all its need.
Nature I worshipped, whose fecundity
Embraces every vision the most fair,
Of perfect benediction. From a boy
I gloated on existence. Earth to me
Seemed all-sufficient and my sojourn there
One trembling opportunity for joy.

Virginibus Puerisque . . .
I care not that one listen if he lives
For aught but life's romance, nor puts above
All life's necessities the need to love,
Nor counts his greatest wealth what Beauty gives.
But sometime on an afternoon in spring,
When dandelions dot the fields with gold,
And under rustling shade a few weeks old
'Tis sweet to stroll and hear the bluebirds sing,
Do you, blond head, whom beauty and the power
Of being young and winsome have prepared
For life's last privilege that really pays,
Make the companion of an idle hour
These relics of the time when I too fared
Across the sweet fifth lustrum of my days.

With a Copy of Shakespeare's Sonnets on Leaving College
As one of some fat tillage dispossessed,
Weighing the yield of these four faded years,
If any ask what fruit seems loveliest,
What lasting gold among the garnered ears,
Ah, then I'll say what hours I had of thine,
Therein I reaped Time's richest revenue,
Read in thy text the sense of David's line,
Through thee achieved the love that Shakespeare knew.
Take then his book, laden with mine own love
As flowers made sweeter by deep-drunken rain,
That when years sunder and between us move
Wide waters, and less kindly bonds constrain,
Thou may'st turn here, dear boy, and reading see
Some part of what thy friend once felt for thee.

Written in a Volume of the Comtesse de Noailles

Be my companion under cool arcades
That frame some drowsy street and dazzling square
Beyond whose flowers and palm-tree promenades
White belfries burn in the blue tropic air.
Lie near me in dim forests where the croon
Of wood-doves sounds and moss-banked water flows,
Or musing late till the midsummer moon
Breaks through some ruined abbey's empty rose.
Sweetest of those to-day whose pious hands
Tend the sequestered altar of Romance,
Where fewer offerings burn, and fewer kneel,
Pour there your passionate beauty on my heart,
And, gladdening such solitudes, impart
How sweet the fellowship of those who feel!

Coucy
The rooks aclamor when one enters here
Startle the empty towers far overhead;
Through gaping walls the summer fields appear,
Green, tan, or, poppy-mingled, tinged with red.
The courts where revel rang deep grass and moss
Cover, and tangled vines have overgrown
The gate where banners blazoned with a cross
Rolled forth to toss round Tyre and Ascalon.
Decay consumes it. The old causes fade.
And fretting for the contest many a heart
Waits their Tyrtaeus to chant on the new.
Oh, pass him by who, in this haunted shade
Musing enthralled, has only this much art,
To love the things the birds and flowers love too.

Tezcotzinco
Though thou art now a ruin bare and cold,
Thou wert sometime the garden of a king.
The birds have sought a lovelier place to sing.
The flowers are few. It was not so of old.
It was not thus when hand in hand there strolled
Through arbors perfumed with undying Spring
Bare bodies beautiful, brown, glistening,
Decked with green plumes and rings of yellow gold.
Do you suppose the herdsman sometimes hears
Vague echoes borne beneath the moon's pale ray
From those old, old, far-off, forgotten years?
Who knows? Here where his ancient kings held sway
He stands. Their names are strangers to his ears.
Even their memory has passed away.

The Old Lowe House, Staten Island

Another prospect pleased the builder's eye,
And Fashion tenanted (where Fashion wanes)
Here in the sorrowful suburban lanes
When first these gables rose against the sky.
Relic of a romantic taste gone by,
This stately monument alone remains,
Vacant, with lichened walls and window-panes
Blank as the windows of a skull. But I,
On evenings when autumnal winds have stirred
In the porch-vines, to this gray oracle
Have laid a wondering ear and oft-times heard,
As from the hollow of a stranded shell,
Old voices echoing (or my fancy erred)
Things indistinct, but not insensible.

Oneata
A hilltop sought by every soothing breeze
That loves the melody of murmuring boughs,
Cool shades, green acreage, and antique house
Fronting the ocean and the dawn; than these
Old monks built never for the spirit's ease
Cloisters more calm not Cluny nor Clairvaux;
Sweet are the noises from the bay below,
And cuckoos calling in the tulip-trees.
Here, a yet empty suitor in thy train,
Beloved Poesy, great joy was mine
To while a listless spell of summer days,
Happier than hoarder in each evening's gain,
When evenings found me richer by one line,
One verse well turned, or serviceable phrase.

On the Cliffs, Newport
Tonight a shimmer of gold lies mantled o'er
Smooth lovely Ocean. Through the lustrous gloom
A savor steals from linden trees in bloom
And gardens ranged at many a palace door.
Proud walls rise here, and, where the moonbeams pour
Their pale enchantment down the dim coast-line,
Terrace and lawn, trim hedge and flowering vine,
Crown with fair culture all the sounding shore.
How sweet, to such a place, on such a night,
From halls with beauty and festival a-glare,
To come distract and, stretched on the cool turf,
Yield to some fond, improbable delight,
While the moon, reddening, sinks, and all the air
Sighs with the muffled tumult of the surf!

To England at the Outbreak of the Balkan War

A cloud has lowered that shall not soon pass o'er.
The world takes sides: whether for impious aims
With Tyranny whose bloody toll enflames
A generous people to heroic war;
Whether with Freedom, stretched in her own gore,
Whose pleading hands and suppliant distress
Still offer hearts that thirst for Righteousness
A glorious cause to strike or perish for.
England, which side is thine? Thou hast had sons
Would shrink not from the choice however grim,
Were Justice trampled on and Courage downed;
Which will they be - cravens or champions?
Oh, if a doubt intrude, remember him
Whose death made Missolonghi holy ground.

At the Tomb of Napoleon Before the Elections in America - November, 1912
I stood beside his sepulchre whose fame,
Hurled over Europe once on bolt and blast,
Now glows far off as storm-clouds overpast
Glow in the sunset flushed with glorious flame.
Has Nature marred his mould? Can Art acclaim
No hero now, no man with whom men side
As with their hearts' high needs personified?
There are will say, One such our lips could name;
Columbia gave him birth. Him Genius most
Gifted to rule. Against the world's great man
Lift their low calumny and sneering cries
The Pharisaic multitude, the host
Of piddling slanderers whose little eyes
Know not what greatness is and never can.

The Rendezvous
He faints with hope and fear. It is the hour.
Distant, across the thundering organ-swell,
In sweet discord from the cathedral-tower,
Fall the faint chimes and the thrice-sequent bell.
Over the crowd his eye uneasy roves.
He sees a plume, a fur; his heart dilates
Soars . . . and then sinks again. It is not hers he loves.
She will not come, the woman that he waits.

Braided with streams of silver incense rise
The antique prayers and ponderous antiphones.
'Gloria Patri' echoes to the skies;
'Nunc et in saecula' the choir intones.
He marks not the monotonous refrain,
The priest that serves nor him that celebrates,
But ever scans the aisle for his blonde head. . . . In vain!
She will not come, the woman that he waits.

How like a flower seemed the perfumed place
Where the sweet flesh lay loveliest to kiss;
And her white hands in what delicious ways,
With what unfeigned caresses, answered his!
Each tender charm intolerable to lose,
Each happy scene his fancy recreates.
And he calls out her name and spreads his arms . . . No use!
She will not come, the woman that he waits.

But the long vespers close. The priest on high
Raises the thing that Christ's own flesh enforms;
And down the Gothic nave the crowd flows by
And through the portal's carven entry swarms.
Maddened he peers upon each passing face
Till the long drab procession terminates.
No princess passes out with proud majestic pace.
She has not come, the woman that he waits.

Back in the empty silent church alone
He walks with aching heart. A white-robed boy
Puts out the altar-candles one by one,
Even as by inches darkens all his joy.
He dreams of the sweet night their lips first met,
And groans and turns to leave and hesitates . . .
Poor stricken heart, he will, he cannot fancy yet
She will not come, the woman that he waits.

But in an arch where deepest shadows fall
He sits and studies the old, storied panes,
And the calm crucifix that from the wall
Looks on a world that quavers and complains.
Hopeless, abandoned, desolate, aghast,
On modes of violent death he meditates.
And the tower-clock tolls five, and he admits at last,
She will not come, the woman that he waits.

Through the stained rose the winter daylight dies,
And all the tide of anguish unrepressed
Swells in his throat and gathers in his eyes;
He kneels and bows his head upon his breast,
And feigns a prayer to hide his burning tears,
While the satanic voice reiterates
'Tonight, tomorrow, nay, nor all the impending years,
She will not come,' the woman that he waits.

Fond, fervent heart of life's enamored spring,
So true, so confident, so passing fair,
That thought of Love as some sweet, tender thing,
And not as war, red tooth and nail laid bare,
How in that hour its innocence was slain,

How from that hour our disillusion dates,
When first we learned thy sense, ironical refrain,
She will not come, the woman that he waits.

Do You Remember Once . . .

I

Do you remember once, in Paris of glad faces,
The night we wandered off under the third moon's rays
And, leaving far behind bright streets and busy places,
Stood where the Seine flowed down between its quiet quais?

The city's voice was hushed; the placid, lustrous waters
Mirrored the walls across where orange windows burned.
Out of the starry south provoking rumors brought us
Far promise of the spring already northward turned.

And breast drew near to breast, and round its soft desire
My arm uncertain stole and clung there unrepelled.
I thought that nevermore my heart would hover nigher
To the last flower of bliss that Nature's garden held.

There, in your beauty's sweet abandonment to pleasure,
The mute, half-open lips and tender, wondering eyes,
I saw embodied first smile back on me the treasure
Long sought across the seas and back of summer skies.

Dear face, when courted Death shall claim my limbs and find them
Laid in some desert place, alone or where the tides
Of war's tumultuous waves on the wet sands behind them
Leave rifts of gasping life when their red flood subsides,

Out of the past's remote delirious abysses
Shine forth once more as then you shone, beloved head,
Laid back in ecstasy between our blinding kisses,
Transfigured with the bliss of being so coveted.

And my sick arms will part, and though hot fever sear it,
My mouth will curve again with the old, tender flame.
And darkness will come down, still finding in my spirit
The dream of your brief love, and on my lips your name.

II

You loved me on that moonlit night long since.
You were my queen and I the charming prince
Elected from a world of mortal men.
You loved me once. . . . What pity was it, then,
You loved not Love. . . . Deep in the emerald west,
Like a returning caravel caressed
By breezes that load all the ambient airs
With clinging fragrance of the bales it bears

From harbors where the caravans come down,
I see over the roof-tops of the town
The new moon back again, but shall not see
The joy that once it had in store for me,
Nor know again the voice upon the stair,
The little studio in the candle-glare,
And all that makes in word and touch and glance
The bliss of the first nights of a romance
When will to love and be beloved casts out
The want to question or the will to doubt.
You loved me once. . . . Under the western seas
The pale moon settles and the Pleiades.
The firelight sinks; outside the night-winds moan
The hour advances, and I sleep alone.

III
Farewell, dear heart, enough of vain despairing!
If I have erred I plead but one excuse
The jewel were a lesser joy in wearing
That cost a lesser agony to lose.

I had not bid for beautifuller hours
Had I not found the door so near unsealed,
Nor hoped, had you not filled my arms with flowers,
For that one flower that bloomed too far afield.

If I have wept, it was because, forsaken,
I felt perhaps more poignantly than some
The blank eternity from which we waken
And all the blank eternity to come.

And I betrayed how sweet a thing and tender
(In the regret with which my lip was curled)
Seemed in its tragic, momentary splendor
My transit through the beauty of the world.

The Bayadere
Flaked, drifting clouds hide not the full moon's rays
More than her beautiful bright limbs were hid
By the light veils they burned and blushed amid,
Skilled to provoke in soft, lascivious ways,
And there was invitation in her voice
And laughing lips and wonderful dark eyes,
As though above the gates of Paradise
Fair verses bade, Be welcome and rejoice!

O'er rugs where mottled blue and green and red
Blent in the patterns of the Orient loom,
Like a bright butterfly from bloom to bloom,
She floated with delicious arms outspread.

There was no pose she took, no move she made,
But all the feverous, love-envenomed flesh
Wrapped round as in the gladiator's mesh
And smote as with his triple-forked blade.

I thought that round her sinuous beauty curled
Fierce exhalations of hot human love,
Around her beauty valuable above
The sunny outspread kingdoms of the world;
Flowing as ever like a dancing fire
Flowed her belled ankles and bejewelled wrists,
Around her beauty swept like sanguine mists
The nimbus of a thousand hearts' desire.

Eudaemon
O happiness, I know not what far seas,
Blue hills and deep, thy sunny realms surround,
That thus in Music's wistful harmonies
And concert of sweet sound
A rumor steals, from some uncertain shore,
Of lovely things outworn or gladness yet in store:

Whether thy beams be pitiful and come,
Across the sundering of vanished years,
From childhood and the happy fields of home,
Like eyes instinct with tears
Felt through green brakes of hedge and apple-bough
Round haunts delightful once, desert and silent now;

Or yet if prescience of unrealized love
Startle the breast with each melodious air,
And gifts that gentle hands are donors of
Still wait intact somewhere,
Furled up all golden in a perfumed place
Within the folded petals of forthcoming days.

Only forever, in the old unrest
Of winds and waters and the varying year,
A litany from islands of the blessed
Answers, Not here . . . not here!
And over the wide world that wandering cry
Shall lead my searching heart unsoothed until I die.

Broceliande
Broceliande! in the perilous beauty of silence and menacing shade,
Thou art set on the shores of the sea down the haze
of horizons untravelled, unscanned.
Untroubled, untouched with the woes of this world
are the moon-marshalled hosts that invade

Broceliande.

Only at dusk, when lavender clouds in the orient twilight disband,
Vanishing where all the blue afternoon they have drifted in solemn parade,
Sometimes a whisper comes down on the wind from the valleys of Fairyland

Sometimes an echo most mournful and faint like the horn of a huntsman strayed,
Faint and forlorn, half drowned in the murmur of foliage fitfully fanned,
Breathes in a burden of nameless regret till I startle,
disturbed and affrayed:
Broceliande
Broceliande
Broceliande. . . .

Lyonesse
In Lyonesse was beauty enough, men say:
Long Summer loaded the orchards to excess,
And fertile lowlands lengthening far away,
In Lyonesse.

Came a term to that land's old favoredness:
Past the sea-walls, crumbled in thundering spray,
Rolled the green waves, ravening, merciless.

Through bearded boughs immobile in cool decay,
Where sea-bloom covers corroding palaces,
The mermaid glides with a curious glance to-day,
In Lyonesse.

Tithonus
So when the verdure of his life was shed,
With all the grace of ripened manlihead,
And on his locks, but now so lovable,
Old age like desolating winter fell,
Leaving them white and flowerless and forlorn:
Then from his bed the Goddess of the Morn
Softly withheld, yet cherished him no less
With pious works of pitying tenderness;
Till when at length with vacant, heedless eyes,
And hoary height bent down none otherwise
Than burdened willows bend beneath their weight
Of snow when winter winds turn temperate,
So bowed with years, when still he lingered on:
Then to the daughter of Hyperion
This counsel seemed the best: for she, afar
By dove-gray seas under the morning star,
Where, on the wide world's uttermost extremes,
Her amber-walled, auroral palace gleams,
High in an orient chamber bade prepare

An everlasting couch, and laid him there,
And leaving, closed the shining doors. But he,
Deathless by Jove's compassionless decree,
Found not, as others find, a dreamless rest.
There wakeful, with half-waking dreams oppressed,
Still in an aural, visionary haze
Float round him vanished forms of happier days;
Still at his side he fancies to behold
The rosy, radiant thing beloved of old;
And oft, as over dewy meads at morn,
Far inland from a sunrise coast is borne
The drowsy, muffled moaning of the sea,
Even so his voice flows on unceasingly,
Lisping sweet names of passion overblown,
Breaking with dull, persistent undertone
The breathless silence that forever broods
Round those colossal, lustrous solitudes.
Times change. Man's fortune prospers, or it falls.
Change harbors not in those eternal halls
And tranquil chamber where Tithonus lies.
But through his window there the eastern skies
Fall palely fair to the dim ocean's end.
There, in blue mist where air and ocean blend,
The lazy clouds that sail the wide world o'er
Falter and turn where they can sail no more.
There singing groves, there spacious gardens blow
Cedars and silver poplars, row on row,
Through whose black boughs on her appointed night,
Flooding his chamber with enchanted light,
Lifts the full moon's immeasurable sphere,
Crimson and huge and wonderfully near.

An Ode to Antares
At dusk, when lowlands where dark waters glide
Robe in gray mist, and through the greening hills
The hoot-owl calls his mate, and whippoorwills
Clamor from every copse and orchard-side,
I watched the red star rising in the East,
And while his fellows of the flaming sign
From prisoning daylight more and more released,
Lift their pale lamps, and, climbing higher, higher,
Out of their locks the waters of the Line
Shaking in clouds of phosphorescent fire,
Rose in the splendor of their curving flight,
Their dolphin leap across the austral night,
From windows southward opening on the sea
What eyes, I wondered, might be watching, too,
Orbed in some blossom-laden balcony.
Where, from the garden to the rail above,
As though a lover's greeting to his love

Should borrow body and form and hue
And tower in torrents of floral flame,
The crimson bougainvillea grew,
What starlit brow uplifted to the same
Majestic regress of the summering sky,
What ultimate thing, hushed, holy, throned as high
Above the currents that tarnish and profane
As silver summits are whose pure repose
No curious eyes disclose
Nor any footfalls stain,
But round their beauty on azure evenings
Only the oreads go on gauzy wings,
Only the oreads troop with dance and song
And airy beings in rainbow mists who throng
Out of those wonderful worlds that lie afar
Betwixt the outmost cloud and the nearest star.

Like the moon, sanguine in the orient night
Shines the red flower in her beautiful hair.
Her breasts are distant islands of delight
Upon a sea where all is soft and fair.
Those robes that make a silken sheath
For each lithe attitude that flows beneath,
Shrouding in scented folds sweet warmths and tumid flowers,
Call them far clouds that half emerge
Beyond a sunset ocean's utmost verge,
Hiding in purple shade and downpour of soft showers
Enchanted isles by mortal foot untrod,
And there in humid dells resplendent orchids nod;
There always from serene horizons blow
Soul-easing gales and there all spice-trees grow
That Phoenix robbed to line his fragrant nest
Each hundred years in Araby the Blest.

Star of the South that now through orient mist
At nightfall off Tampico or Belize
Greetest the sailor rising from those seas
Where first in me, a fond romanticist,
The tropic sunset's bloom on cloudy piles
Cast out industrious cares with dreams of fabulous isles
Thou lamp of the swart lover to his tryst,
O'er planted acres at the jungle's rim
Reeking with orange-flower and tuberose,
Dear to his eyes thy ruddy splendor glows
Among the palms where beauty waits for him;
Bliss too thou bringst to our greening North,
Red scintillant through cherry-blossom rifts,
Herald of summer-heat, and all the gifts
And all the joys a summer can bring forth

Be thou my star, for I have made my aim

To follow loveliness till autumn-strown
Sunder the sinews of this flower-like frame
As rose-leaves sunder when the bud is blown.
Ay, sooner spirit and sense disintegrate
Than reconcilement to a common fate
Strip the enchantment from a world so dressed
In hues of high romance. I cannot rest
While aught of beauty in any path untrod
Swells into bloom and spreads sweet charms abroad
Unworshipped of my love. I cannot see
In Life's profusion and passionate brevity
How hearts enamored of life can strain too much
In one long tension to hear, to see, to touch.
Now on each rustling night-wind from the South
Far music calls; beyond the harbor mouth
Each outbound argosy with sail unfurled
May point the path through this fortuitous world
That holds the heart from its desire. Away!
Where tinted coast-towns gleam at close of day,
Where squares are sweet with bells, or shores thick set
With bloom and bower, with mosque and minaret.
Blue peaks loom up beyond the coast-plains here,
White roads wind up the dales and disappear,
By silvery waters in the plains afar
Glimmers the inland city like a star,
With gilded gates and sunny spires ablaze
And burnished domes half-seen through luminous haze,
Lo, with what opportunity Earth teems!
How like a fair its ample beauty seems!
Fluttering with flags its proud pavilions rise:
What bright bazaars, what marvelous merchandise,
Down seething alleys what melodious din,
What clamor importuning from every booth!
At Earth's great market where Joy is trafficked in
Buy while thy purse yet swells with golden Youth!

Translations

Dante. Inferno, Canto XXVI
Florence, rejoice! For thou o'er land and sea
So spread'st thy pinions that the fame of thee
Hath reached no less into the depths of Hell.
So noble were the five I found to dwell
Therein, thy sons, whence shame accrues to me
And no great praise is thine; but if it be
That truth unveil in dreamings before dawn,
Then is the vengeful hour not far withdrawn
When Prato shall exult within her walls
To see thy suffering. Whate'er befalls,

Let it come soon, since come it must, for later,
Each year would see my grief for thee the greater.

We left; and once more up the craggy side
By the blind steps of our descent, my guide,
Remounting, drew me on. So we pursued
The rugged path through that steep solitude,
Where rocks and splintered fragments strewed the land
So thick, that foot availed not without hand.
Grief filled me then, and still great sorrow stirs
My heart as oft as memory recurs
To what I saw; that more and more I rein
My natural powers, and curb them lest they strain
Where Virtue guide not, that if some good star,
Or better thing, have made them what they are,
That good I may not grudge, nor turn to ill.

As when, reclining on some verdant hill
What season the hot sun least veils his power
That lightens all, and in that gloaming hour
The fly resigns to the shrill gnat, even then,
As rustic, looking down, sees, o'er the glen,
Vineyard, or tilth where lies his husbandry,
Fireflies innumerable sparkle: so to me,
Come where its mighty depth unfolded, straight
With flames no fewer seemed to scintillate
The shades of the eighth pit. And as to him
Whose wrongs the bears avenged, dim and more dim
Elijah's chariot seemed, when to the skies
Uprose the heavenly steeds; and still his eyes
Strained, following them, till naught remained in view
But flame, like a thin cloud against the blue:
So here, the melancholy gulf within,
Wandered these flames, concealing each its sin,
Yet each, a fiery integument,
Wrapped round a sinner.

On the bridge intent,
Gazing I stood, and grasped its flinty side,
Or else, unpushed, had fallen. And my guide,
Observing me so moved, spake, saying: "Behold
Where swathed each in his unconsuming fold,
The spirits lie confined." Whom answering,
"Master," I said, "thy words assurance bring
To that which I already had supposed;
And I was fain to ask who lies enclosed
In the embrace of that dividing fire,
Which seems to curl above the fabled pyre,
Where with his twin-born brother, fiercely hated,
Eteocles was laid." He answered, "Mated
In punishment as once in wrath they were,

Ulysses there and Diomed incur
The eternal pains; there groaning they deplore
The ambush of the horse, which made the door
For Rome's imperial seed to issue: there
In anguish too they wail the fatal snare
Whence dead Deidamia still must grieve,
Reft of Achilles; likewise they receive
Due penalty for the Palladium."
"Master," I said, "if in that martyrdom
The power of human speech may still be theirs,
I pray and think it worth a thousand prayers
That, till this horned flame become more nigh,
We may abide here; for thou seest that I
With great desire incline to it." And he:
"Thy prayer deserves great praise; which willingly
I grant; but thou refrain from speaking; leave
That task to me; for fully I conceive
What thing thou wouldst, and it might fall perchance
That these, being Greeks, would scorn thine utterance."

So when the flame had come where time and place
Seemed not unfitting to my guide with grace
To question, thus he spoke at my desire:
"O ye that are two souls within one fire,
If in your eyes some merit I have won
Merit, or more or less, for tribute done
When in the world I framed my lofty verse:
Move not; but fain were we that one rehearse
By what strange fortunes to his death he came."
The elder crescent of the antique flame
Began to wave, as in the upper air
A flame is tempest-tortured, here and there
Tossing its angry height, and in its sound
As human speech it suddenly had found,
Rolled forth a voice of thunder, saying: "When,
The twelvemonth past in Circe's halls, again
I left Gaeta's strand (ere thither came
Aeneas, and had given it that name)
Not love of son, nor filial reverence,
Nor that affection that might recompense
The weary vigil of Penelope,
Could so far quench the hot desire in me
To prove more wonders of the teeming earth,
Of human frailty and of manly worth.
In one small bark, and with the faithful band
That all awards had shared of Fortune's hand,
I launched once more upon the open main.
Both shores I visited as far as Spain,
Sardinia, and Morocco, and what more
The midland sea upon its bosom wore.
The hour of our lives was growing late

When we arrived before that narrow strait
Where Hercules had set his bounds to show
That there Man's foot shall pause, and further none shall go.
Borne with the gale past Seville on the right,
And on the left now swept by Ceuta's site,
'Brothers,' I cried, 'that into the far West
Through perils numberless are now addressed,
In this brief respite that our mortal sense
Yet hath, shrink not from new experience;
But sailing still against the setting sun,
Seek we new worlds where Man has never won
Before us. Ponder your proud destinies:
Born were ye not like brutes for swinish ease,
But virtue and high knowledge to pursue.'
My comrades with such zeal did I imbue
By these brief words, that scarcely could I then
Have turned them from their purpose; so again
We set out poop against the morning sky,
And made our oars as wings wherewith to fly
Into the Unknown. And ever from the right
Our course deflecting, in the balmy night
All southern stars we saw, and ours so low,
That scarce above the sea-marge it might show.
So five revolving periods the soft,
Pale light had robbed of Cynthia, and as oft
Replenished since our start, when far and dim
Over the misty ocean's utmost rim,
Rose a great mountain, that for very height
Passed any I had seen. Boundless delight
Filled us, alas, and quickly turned to dole:
For, springing from our scarce-discovered goal,
A whirlwind struck the ship; in circles three
It whirled us helpless in the eddying sea;
High on the fourth the fragile stern uprose,
The bow drove down, and, as Another chose,
Over our heads we heard the surging billows close."

Ariosto. Orlando Furioso, Canto X, 91-99
Ruggiero, to amaze the British host,
And wake more wonder in their wondering ranks,
The bridle of his winged courser loosed,
And clapped his spurs into the creature's flanks;
High in the air, even to the topmost banks
Of crudded cloud, uprose the flying horse,
And now above the Welsh, and now the Manx,
And now across the sea he shaped his course,
Till gleaming far below lay Erin's emerald shores.

There round Hibernia's fabled realm he coasted,
Where the old saint had left the holy cave,

Sought for the famous virtue that it boasted
To purge the sinful visitor and save.
Thence back returning over land and wave,
Ruggiero came where the blue currents flow,
The shores of Lesser Brittany to lave,
And, looking down while sailing to and fro,
He saw Angelica chained to the rock below.

'Twas on the Island of Complaint, well named,
For there to that inhospitable shore,
A savage people, cruel and untamed,
Brought the rich prize of many a hateful war.
To feed a monster that bestead them sore,
They of fair ladies those that loveliest shone,
Of tender maidens they the tenderest bore,
And, drowned in tears and making piteous moan,
Left for that ravening beast, chained on the rocks alone.

Thither transported by enchanter's art,
Angelica from dreams most innocent
(As the tale mentioned in another part)
Awoke, the victim for that sad event.
Beauty so rare, nor birth so excellent,
Nor tears that make sweet Beauty lovelier still,
Could turn that people from their harsh intent.
Alas, what temper is conceived so ill
But, Pity moving not, Love's soft enthralment will?

On the cold granite at the ocean's rim
These folk had chained her fast and gone their way;
Fresh in the softness of each delicate limb
The pity of their bruising violence lay.
Over her beauty, from the eye of day
To hide its pleading charms, no veil was thrown.
Only the fragments of the salt sea-spray
Rose from the churning of the waves, wind-blown,
To dash upon a whiteness creamier than their own.

Carved out of candid marble without flaw,
Or alabaster blemishless and rare,
Ruggiero might have fancied what he saw,
For statue-like it seemed, and fastened there
By craft of cunningest artificer;
Save in the wistful eyes Ruggiero thought
A teardrop gleamed, and with the rippling hair
The ocean breezes played as if they sought
In its loose depths to hide that which her hand might not.

Pity and wonder and awakening love
Strove in the bosom of the Moorish Knight.
Down from his soaring in the skies above

He urged the tenor of his courser's flight.
Fairer with every foot of lessening height
Shone the sweet prisoner. With tightening reins
He drew more nigh, and gently as he might:
"O lady, worthy only of the chains
With which his bounden slaves the God of Love constrains,

"And least for this or any ill designed,
Oh, what unnatural and perverted race
Could the sweet flesh with flushing stricture bind,
And leave to suffer in this cold embrace
That the warm arms so hunger to replace?"
Into the damsel's cheeks such color flew
As by the alchemy of ancient days
If whitest ivory should take the hue
Of coral where it blooms deep in the liquid blue.

Nor yet so tightly drawn the cruel chains
Clasped the slim ankles and the wounded hands,
But with soft, cringing attitudes in vain
She strove to shield her from that ardent glance.
So, clinging to the walls of some old manse,
The rose-vine strives to shield her tender flowers,
When the rude wind, as autumn weeks advance,
Beats on the walls and whirls about the towers
And spills at every blast her pride in piteous showers.

And first for choking sobs she might not speak,
And then, "Alas!" she cried, "ah, woe is me!"
And more had said in accents faint and weak,
Pleading for succor and sweet liberty.
But hark! across the wide ways of the sea
Rose of a sudden such a fierce affray
That any but the brave had turned to flee.
Ruggiero, turning, looked. To his dismay,
Lo, where the monster came to claim his quivering prey!

On a Theme in the Greek Anthology
Thy petals yet are closely curled,
Rose of the world,
Around their scented, golden core;
Nor yet has Summer purpled o'er
Thy tender clusters that begin
To swell within
The dewy vine-leaves' early screen
Of sheltering green.

O hearts that are Love's helpless prey,
While yet you may,
Fly, ere the shaft is on the string!

The fire that now is smouldering
Shall be the conflagration soon
Whose paths are strewn
With torment of blanched lips and eyes
That agonize.

After an Epigram of Clement Marot
The lad I was I longer now
Nor am nor shall be evermore.
Spring's lovely blossoms from my brow
Have shed their petals on the floor.
Thou, Love, hast been my lord, thy shrine
Above all gods' best served by me.
Dear Love, could life again be mine
How bettered should that service be!

Last Poems

1916

The Aisne (1914-15)
We first saw fire on the tragic slopes
Where the flood-tide of France's early gain,
Big with wrecked promise and abandoned hopes,
Broke in a surf of blood along the Aisne.

The charge her heroes left us, we assumed,
What, dying, they reconquered, we preserved,
In the chill trenches, harried, shelled, entombed,
Winter came down on us, but no man swerved.

Winter came down on us. The low clouds, torn
In the stark branches of the riven pines,
Blurred the white rockets that from dusk till morn
Traced the wide curve of the close-grappling lines.

In rain, and fog that on the withered hill
Froze before dawn, the lurking foe drew down;
Or light snows fell that made forlorner still
The ravaged country and the ruined town;

Or the long clouds would end. Intensely fair,
The winter constellations blazing forth
Perseus, the Twins, Orion, the Great Bear
Gleamed on our bayonets pointing to the north.

And the lone sentinel would start and soar
On wings of strong emotion as he knew

That kinship with the stars that only War
Is great enough to lift man's spirit to.

And ever down the curving front, aglow
With the pale rockets' intermittent light,
He heard, like distant thunder, growl and grow
The rumble of far battles in the night,

Rumors, reverberant, indistinct, remote,
Borne from red fields whose martial names have won
The power to thrill like a far trumpet-note,
Vic, Vailly, Soupir, Hurtelise, Craonne. . .

Craonne, before thy cannon-swept plateau,
Where like sere leaves lay strewn September's dead,
I found for all dear things I forfeited
A recompense I would not now forego.

For that high fellowship was ours then
With those who, championing another's good,
More than dull Peace or its poor votaries could,
Taught us the dignity of being men.

There we drained deeper the deep cup of life,
And on sublimer summits came to learn,
After soft things, the terrible and stern,
After sweet Love, the majesty of Strife;

There where we faced under those frowning heights
The blast that maims, the hurricane that kills;
There where the watchlights on the winter hills
Flickered like balefire through inclement nights;

There where, firm links in the unyielding chain,
Where fell the long-planned blow and fell in vain
Hearts worthy of the honor and the trial,
We helped to hold the lines along the Aisne.

Champagne (1914-15)
In the glad revels, in the happy fetes,
When cheeks are flushed, and glasses gilt and pearled
With the sweet wine of France that concentrates
The sunshine and the beauty of the world,

Drink sometimes, you whose footsteps yet may tread
The undisturbed, delightful paths of Earth,
To those whose blood, in pious duty shed,
Hallows the soil where that same wine had birth.

Here, by devoted comrades laid away,

Along our lines they slumber where they fell,
Beside the crater at the Ferme d'Alger
And up the bloody slopes of La Pompelle,

And round the city whose cathedral towers
The enemies of Beauty dared profane,
And in the mat of multicolored flowers
That clothe the sunny chalk-fields of Champagne.

Under the little crosses where they rise
The soldier rests. Now round him undismayed
The cannon thunders, and at night he lies
At peace beneath the eternal fusillade. . . .

That other generations might possess
From shame and menace free in years to come
A richer heritage of happiness,
He marched to that heroic martyrdom.

Esteeming less the forfeit that he paid
Than undishonored that his flag might float
Over the towers of liberty, he made
His breast the bulwark and his blood the moat.

Obscurely sacrificed, his nameless tomb,
Bare of the sculptor's art, the poet's lines,
Summer shall flush with poppy-fields in bloom,
And Autumn yellow with maturing vines.

There the grape-pickers at their harvesting
Shall lightly tread and load their wicker trays,
Blessing his memory as they toil and sing
In the slant sunshine of October days. . . .

I love to think that if my blood should be
So privileged to sink where his has sunk,
I shall not pass from Earth entirely,
But when the banquet rings, when healths are drunk,

And faces that the joys of living fill
Glow radiant with laughter and good cheer,
In beaming cups some spark of me shall still
Brim toward the lips that once I held so dear.

So shall one coveting no higher plane
Than nature clothes in color and flesh and tone,
Even from the grave put upward to attain
The dreams youth cherished and missed and might have known;

And that strong need that strove unsatisfied
Toward earthly beauty in all forms it wore,

Not death itself shall utterly divide
From the beloved shapes it thirsted for.

Alas, how many an adept for whose arms
Life held delicious offerings perished here,
How many in the prime of all that charms,
Crowned with all gifts that conquer and endear!

Honor them not so much with tears and flowers,
But you with whom the sweet fulfilment lies,
Where in the anguish of atrocious hours
Turned their last thoughts and closed their dying eyes,

Rather when music on bright gatherings lays
Its tender spell, and joy is uppermost,
Be mindful of the men they were, and raise
Your glasses to them in one silent toast.

Drink to them, amorous of dear Earth as well,
They asked no tribute lovelier than this
And in the wine that ripened where they fell,
Oh, frame your lips as though it were a kiss.

Champagne, France, July, 1915.

The Hosts
Purged, with the life they left, of all
That makes life paltry and mean and small,
In their new dedication charged
With something heightened, enriched, enlarged,
That lends a light to their lusty brows
And a song to the rhythm of their tramping feet,
These are the men that have taken vows,
These are the hardy, the flower, the elite,
These are the men that are moved no more
By the will to traffic and grasp and store
And ring with pleasure and wealth and love
The circles that self is the center of;
But they are moved by the powers that force
The sea forever to ebb and rise,
That hold Arcturus in his course,
And marshal at noon in tropic skies
The clouds that tower on some snow-capped chain
And drift out over the peopled plain.
They are big with the beauty of cosmic things.
Mark how their columns surge! They seem
To follow the goddess with outspread wings
That points toward Glory, the soldier's dream.
With bayonets bare and flags unfurled,
They scale the summits of the world

And fade on the farthest golden height
In fair horizons full of light.

Comrades in arms there - friend or foe
That trod the perilous, toilsome trail
Through a world of ruin and blood and woe
In the years of the great decision - hail!
Friend or foe, it shall matter nought;
This only matters, in fine: we fought.
For we were young and in love or strife
Sought exultation and craved excess:
To sound the wildest debauch in life
We staked our youth and its loveliness.
Let idlers argue the right and wrong
And weigh what merit our causes had.
Putting our faith in being strong
Above the level of good and bad
For us, we battled and burned and killed
Because evolving Nature willed,
And it was our pride and boast to be
The instruments of Destiny.
There was a stately drama writ
By the hand that peopled the earth and air
And set the stars in the infinite
And made night gorgeous and morning fair,
And all that had sense to reason knew
That bloody drama must be gone through.
Some sat and watched how the action veered
Waited, profited, trembled, cheered
We saw not clearly nor understood,
But yielding ourselves to the masterhand,
Each in his part as best he could,
We played it through as the author planned.

Maktoob
A shell surprised our post one day
And killed a comrade at my side.
My heart was sick to see the way
He suffered as he died.

I dug about the place he fell,
And found, no bigger than my thumb,
A fragment of the splintered shell
In warm aluminum.

I melted it, and made a mould,
And poured it in the opening,
And worked it, when the cast was cold,
Into a shapely ring.

And when my ring was smooth and bright,
Holding it on a rounded stick,
For seal, I bade a Turco write
'Maktoob' in Arabic.

'Maktoob!' "'Tis written!" . . . So they think,
These children of the desert, who
From its immense expanses drink
Some of its grandeur too.

Within the book of Destiny,
Whose leaves are time, whose cover, space,
The day when you shall cease to be,
The hour, the mode, the place,

Are marked, they say; and you shall not
By taking thought or using wit
Alter that certain fate one jot,
Postpone or conjure it.

Learn to drive fear, then, from your heart.
If you must perish, know, O man,
'Tis an inevitable part
Of the predestined plan.

And, seeing that through the ebon door
Once only you may pass, and meet
Of those that have gone through before
The mighty, the elite

Guard that not bowed nor blanched with fear
You enter, but serene, erect,
As you would wish most to appear
To those you most respect.

So die as though your funeral
Ushered you through the doors that led
Into a stately banquet hall
Where heroes banqueted;

And it shall all depend therein
Whether you come as slave or lord,
If they acclaim you as their kin
Or spurn you from their board.

So, when the order comes: "Attack!"
And the assaulting wave deploys,
And the heart trembles to look back
On life and all its joys;

Or in a ditch that they seem near

To find, and round your shallow trough
Drop the big shells that you can hear
Coming a half mile off;

When, not to hear, some try to talk,
And some to clean their guns, or sing,
And some dig deeper in the chalk
I look upon my ring:

And nerves relax that were most tense,
And Death comes whistling down unheard,
As I consider all the sense
Held in that mystic word.

And it brings, quieting like balm
My heart whose flutterings have ceased,
The resignation and the calm
And wisdom of the East.

I Have a Rendezvous with Death . . .
I have a rendezvous with Death
At some disputed barricade,
When Spring comes back with rustling shade
And apple-blossoms fill the air
I have a rendezvous with Death
When Spring brings back blue days and fair.

It may be he shall take my hand
And lead me into his dark land
And close my eyes and quench my breath
It may be I shall pass him still.
I have a rendezvous with Death
On some scarred slope of battered hill,
When Spring comes round again this year
And the first meadow-flowers appear.

God knows 'twere better to be deep
Pillowed in silk and scented down,
Where Love throbs out in blissful sleep,
Pulse nigh to pulse, and breath to breath,
Where hushed awakenings are dear . . .
But I've a rendezvous with Death
At midnight in some flaming town,
When Spring trips north again this year,
And I to my pledged word am true,
I shall not fail that rendezvous.

Sonnets:

"Sonnet I"
Sidney, in whom the heyday of romance
Came to its precious and most perfect flower,
Whether you tourneyed with victorious lance
Or brought sweet roundelays to Stella's bower,
I give myself some credit for the way
I have kept clean of what enslaves and lowers,
Shunned the ideals of our present day
And studied those that were esteemed in yours;
For, turning from the mob that buys Success
By sacrificing all Life's better part,
Down the free roads of human happiness
I frolicked, poor of purse but light of heart,
And lived in strict devotion all along
To my three idols - Love and Arms and Song.

"Sonnet II"
Not that I always struck the proper mean
Of what mankind must give for what they gain,
But, when I think of those whom dull routine
And the pursuit of cheerless toil enchain,
Who from their desk-chairs seeing a summer cloud
Race through blue heaven on its joyful course
Sigh sometimes for a life less cramped and bowed,
I think I might have done a great deal worse;
For I have ever gone untied and free,
The stars and my high thoughts for company;
Wet with the salt-spray and the mountain showers,
I have had the sense of space and amplitude,
And love in many places, silver-shoed,
Has come and scattered all my path with flowers.

"Sonnet III"
Why should you be astonished that my heart,
Plunged for so long in darkness and in dearth,
Should be revived by you, and stir and start
As by warm April now, reviving Earth?
I am the field of undulating grass
And you the gentle perfumed breath of Spring,
And all my lyric being, when you pass,
Is bowed and filled with sudden murmuring.
I asked you nothing and expected less,
But, with that deep, impassioned tenderness
Of one approaching what he most adores,
I only wished to lose a little space
All thought of my own life, and in its place
To live and dream and have my joy in yours.

"Sonnet IV"
To . . . in church

If I was drawn here from a distant place,
'Twas not to pray nor hear our friend's address,
But, gazing once more on your winsome face,
To worship there Ideal Loveliness.
On that pure shrine that has too long ignored
The gifts that once I brought so frequently
I lay this votive offering, to record
How sweet your quiet beauty seemed to me.
Enchanting girl, my faith is not a thing
By futile prayers and vapid psalm-singing
To vent in crowded nave and public pew.
My creed is simple: that the world is fair,
And beauty the best thing to worship there,
And I confess it by adoring you.

Biarritz, Sunday, March 26, 1916.

"Sonnet V"
Seeing you have not come with me, nor spent
This day's suggestive beauty as we ought,
I have gone forth alone and been content
To make you mistress only of my thought.
And I have blessed the fate that was so kind
In my life's agitations to include
This moment's refuge where my sense can find
Refreshment, and my soul beatitude.
Oh, be my gentle love a little while!
Walk with me sometimes. Let me see you smile.
Watching some night under a wintry sky,
Before the charge, or on the bed of pain,
These blessed memories shall revive again
And be a power to cheer and fortify.

"Sonnet VI"
Oh, you are more desirable to me
Than all I staked in an impulsive hour,
Making my youth the sport of chance, to be
Blighted or torn in its most perfect flower;
For I think less of what that chance may bring
Than how, before returning into fire,
To make my dearest memory of the thing
That is but now my ultimate desire.
And in old times I should have prayed to her
Whose haunt the groves of windy Cyprus were,
To prosper me and crown with good success

My will to make of you the rose-twined bowl
From whose inebriating brim my soul
Shall drink its last of earthly happiness.

"Sonnet VII"
There have been times when I could storm and plead,
But you shall never hear me supplicate.
These long months that have magnified my need
Have made my asking less importunate,
For now small favors seem to me so great
That not the courteous lovers of old time
Were more content to rule themselves and wait,
Easing desire with discourse and sweet rhyme.
Nay, be capricious, willful; have no fear
To wound me with unkindness done or said,
Lest mutual devotion make too dear
My life that hangs by a so slender thread,
And happy love unnerve me before May
For that stern part that I have yet to play.

"Sonnet VIII"
Oh, love of woman, you are known to be
A passion sent to plague the hearts of men;
For every one you bring felicity
Bringing rebuffs and wretchedness to ten.
I have been oft where human life sold cheap
And seen men's brains spilled out about their ears
And yet that never cost me any sleep;
I lived untroubled and I shed no tears.
Fools prate how war is an atrocious thing;
I always knew that nothing it implied
Equalled the agony of suffering
Of him who loves and loves unsatisfied.
War is a refuge to a heart like this;
Love only tells it what true torture is.

"Sonnet IX"
Well, seeing I have no hope, then let us part;
Having long taught my flesh to master fear,
I should have learned by now to rule my heart,
Although, Heaven knows, 'tis not so easy near.
Oh, you were made to make men miserable
And torture those who would have joy in you,
But I, who could have loved you, dear, so well,
Take pride in being a good loser too;
And it has not been wholly unsuccess,
For I have rescued from forgetfulness
Some moments of this precious time that flies,

Adding to my past wealth of memory
The pretty way you once looked up at me,
Your low, sweet voice, your smile, and your dear eyes.

"Sonnet X"
I have sought Happiness, but it has been
A lovely rainbow, baffling all pursuit,
And tasted Pleasure, but it was a fruit
More fair of outward hue than sweet within.
Renouncing both, a flake in the ferment
Of battling hosts that conquer or recoil,
There only, chastened by fatigue and toil,
I knew what came the nearest to content.
For there at least my troubled flesh was free
From the gadfly Desire that plagued it so;
Discord and Strife were what I used to know,
Heartaches, deception, murderous jealousy;
By War transported far from all of these,
Amid the clash of arms I was at peace.

"Sonnet XI"
On Returning to the Front after Leave

Apart sweet women (for whom Heaven be blessed),
Comrades, you cannot think how thin and blue
Look the leftovers of mankind that rest,
Now that the cream has been skimmed off in you.
War has its horrors, but has this of good
That its sure processes sort out and bind
Brave hearts in one intrepid brotherhood
And leave the shams and imbeciles behind.
Now turn we joyful to the great attacks,
Not only that we face in a fair field
Our valiant foe and all his deadly tools,
But also that we turn disdainful backs
On that poor world we scorn yet die to shield
That world of cowards, hypocrites, and fools.

"Sonnet XII"
Clouds rosy-tinted in the setting sun,
Depths of the azure eastern sky between,
Plains where the poplar-bordered highways run,
Patched with a hundred tints of brown and green,
Beauty of Earth, when in thy harmonies
The cannon's note has ceased to be a part,
I shall return once more and bring to these
The worship of an undivided heart.
Of those sweet potentialities that wait

For my heart's deep desire to fecundate
I shall resume the search, if Fortune grants;
And the great cities of the world shall yet
Be golden frames for me in which to set
New masterpieces of more rare romance.

Bellinglise

I

Deep in the sloping forest that surrounds
The head of a green valley that I know,
Spread the fair gardens and ancestral grounds
Of Bellinglise, the beautiful chateau.
Through shady groves and fields of unmown grass,
It was my joy to come at dusk and see,
Filling a little pond's untroubled glass,
Its antique towers and mouldering masonry.
Oh, should I fall to-morrow, lay me here,
That o'er my tomb, with each reviving year,
Wood-flowers may blossom and the wood-doves croon;
And lovers by that unrecorded place,
Passing, may pause, and cling a little space,
Close-bosomed, at the rising of the moon.

II

Here, where in happier times the huntsman's horn
Echoing from far made sweet midsummer eves,
Now serried cannon thunder night and morn,
Tearing with iron the greenwood's tender leaves.
Yet has sweet Spring no particle withdrawn
Of her old bounty; still the song-birds hail,
Even through our fusillade, delightful Dawn;
Even in our wire bloom lilies of the vale.
You who love flowers, take these; their fragile bells
Have trembled with the shock of volleyed shells,
And in black nights when stealthy foes advance
They have been lit by the pale rockets' glow
That o'er scarred fields and ancient towns laid low
Trace in white fire the brave frontiers of France.

May 22, 1916.

Liebestod

I who, conceived beneath another star,
Had been a prince and played with life, instead
Have been its slave, an outcast exiled far
From the fair things my faith has merited.
My ways have been the ways that wanderers tread
And those that make romance of poverty
Soldier, I shared the soldier's board and bed,

And Joy has been a thing more oft to me
Whispered by summer wind and summer sea
Than known incarnate in the hours it lies
All warm against our hearts and laughs into our eyes.

I know not if in risking my best days
I shall leave utterly behind me here
This dream that lightened me through lonesome ways
And that no disappointment made less dear;
Sometimes I think that, where the hilltops rear
Their white entrenchments back of tangled wire,
Behind the mist Death only can make clear,
There, like Brunhilde ringed with flaming fire,
Lies what shall ease my heart's immense desire:
There, where beyond the horror and the pain
Only the brave shall pass, only the strong attain.

Truth or delusion, be it as it may,
Yet think it true, dear friends, for, thinking so,
That thought shall nerve our sinews on the day
When to the last assault our bugles blow:
Reckless of pain and peril we shall go,
Heads high and hearts aflame and bayonets bare,
And we shall brave eternity as though
Eyes looked on us in which we would seem fair
One waited in whose presence we would wear,
Even as a lover who would be well-seen,
Our manhood faultless and our honor clean.

Resurgam
Exiled afar from youth and happy love,
If Death should ravish my fond spirit hence
I have no doubt but, like a homing dove,
It would return to its dear residence,
And through a thousand stars find out the road
Back into earthly flesh that was its loved abode.

A Message to America
You have the grit and the guts, I know;
You are ready to answer blow for blow
You are virile, combative, stubborn, hard,
But your honor ends with your own back-yard;
Each man intent on his private goal,
You have no feeling for the whole;
What singly none would tolerate
You let unpunished hit the state,
Unmindful that each man must share
The stain he lets his country wear,
And (what no traveller ignores)

That her good name is often yours.

You are proud in the pride that feels its might;
From your imaginary height
Men of another race or hue
Are men of a lesser breed to you:
The neighbor at your southern gate
You treat with the scorn that has bred his hate.
To lend a spice to your disrespect
You call him the "greaser". But reflect!
The greaser has spat on you more than once;
He has handed you multiple affronts;
He has robbed you, banished you, burned and killed;
He has gone untrounced for the blood he spilled;
He has jeering used for his bootblack's rag
The stars and stripes of the gringo's flag;
And you, in the depths of your easy-chair
What did you do, what did you care?
Did you find the season too cold and damp
To change the counter for the camp?
Were you frightened by fevers in Mexico?
I can't imagine, but this I know
You are impassioned vastly more
By the news of the daily baseball score
Than to hear that a dozen countrymen
Have perished somewhere in Darien,
That greasers have taken their innocent lives
And robbed their holdings and raped their wives.

Not by rough tongues and ready fists
Can you hope to jilt in the modern lists.
The armies of a littler folk
Shall pass you under the victor's yoke,
Sobeit a nation that trains her sons
To ride their horses and point their guns
Sobeit a people that comprehends
The limit where private pleasure ends
And where their public dues begin,
A people made strong by discipline
Who are willing to give, what you've no mind to
And understand what you are blind to
The things that the individual
Must sacrifice for the good of all.

You have a leader who knows - the man
Most fit to be called American,
A prophet that once in generations
Is given to point to erring nations
Brighter ideals toward which to press
And lead them out of the wilderness.
Will you turn your back on him once again?

Will you give the tiller once more to men
Who have made your country the laughing-stock
For the older peoples to scorn and mock,
Who would make you servile, despised, and weak,
A country that turns the other cheek,
Who care not how bravely your flag may float,
Who answer an insult with a note,
Whose way is the easy way in all,
And, seeing that polished arms appal
Their marrow of milk-fed pacifist,
Would tell you menace does not exist?
Are these, in the world's great parliament,
The men you would choose to represent
Your honor, your manhood, and your pride,
And the virtues your fathers dignified?
Oh, bury them deeper than the sea
In universal obloquy;
Forget the ground where they lie, or write
For epitaph: "Too proud to fight."

I have been too long from my country's shores
To reckon what state of mind is yours,
But as for myself I know right well
I would go through fire and shot and shell
And face new perils and make my bed
In new privations, if ROOSEVELT led;
But I have given my heart and hand
To serve, in serving another land,
Ideals kept bright that with you are dim;
Here men can thrill to their country's hymn,
For the passion that wells in the Marseillaise
Is the same that fires the French these days,
And, when the flag that they love goes by,
With swelling bosom and moistened eye
They can look, for they know that it floats there still
By the might of their hands and the strength of their will,
And through perils countless and trials unknown
Its honor each man has made his own.
They wanted the war no more than you,
But they saw how the certain menace grew,
And they gave two years of their youth or three
The more to insure their liberty
When the wrath of rifles and pennoned spears
Should roll like a flood on their wrecked frontiers.
They wanted the war no more than you,
But when the dreadful summons blew
And the time to settle the quarrel came
They sprang to their guns, each man was game;
And mark if they fight not to the last
For their hearths, their altars, and their past:
Yea, fight till their veins have been bled dry

For love of the country that WILL not die.

O friends, in your fortunate present ease
(Yet faced by the self-same facts as these),
If you would see how a race can soar
That has no love, but no fear, of war,
How each can turn from his private role
That all may act as a perfect whole,
How men can live up to the place they claim
And a nation, jealous of its good name,
Be true to its proud inheritance,
Oh, look over here and learn from FRANCE!

Introduction and Conclusion of a Long Poem
I have gone sometimes by the gates of Death
And stood beside the cavern through whose doors
Enter the voyagers into the unseen.
From that dread threshold only, gazing back,
Have eyes in swift illumination seen
Life utterly revealed, and guessed therein
What things were vital and what things were vain.
Know then, like a vast ocean from my feet
Spreading away into the morning sky,
I saw unrolled my vanished days, and, lo,
Oblivion like a morning mist obscured
Toils, trials, ambitions, agitations, ease,
And like green isles, sun-kissed, with sweet perfume
Loading the airs blown back from that dim gulf,
Gleamed only through the all-involving haze
The hours when we have loved and been beloved.

Therefore, sweet friends, as often as by Love
You rise absorbed into the harmony
Of planets singing round magnetic suns,
Let not propriety nor prejudice
Nor the precepts of jealous age deny
What Sense so incontestably affirms;
Cling to the blessed moment and drink deep
Of the sweet cup it tends, as there alone
Were that which makes life worth the pain to live.
What is so fair as lovers in their joy
That dies in sleep, their sleep that wakes in joy?
Caressing arms are their light pillows. They
That like lost stars have wandered hitherto
Lonesome and lightless through the universe,
Now glow transfired at Nature's flaming core;
They are the centre; constellated heaven
Is the embroidered panoply spread round
Their bridal, and the music of the spheres
Rocks them in hushed epithalamium.

I know that there are those whose idle tongues
Blaspheme the beauty of the world that was
So wondrous and so worshipful to me.
I call them those that, in the palace where
Down perfumed halls the Sleeping Beauty lay,
Wandered without the secret or the key.
I know that there are those, of gentler heart,
Broken by grief or by deception bowed,
Who in some realm beyond the grave conceive
The bliss they found not here; but, as for me,
In the soft fibres of the tender flesh
I saw potentialities of Joy
Ten thousand lifetimes could not use. Dear Earth,
In this dark month when deep as morning dew
On thy maternal breast shall fall the blood
Of those that were thy loveliest and thy best,
If it be fate that mine shall mix with theirs,
Hear this my natural prayer, for, purified
By that Lethean agony and clad
In more resplendent powers, I ask nought else
Than reincarnate to retrace my path,
Be born again of woman, walk once more
Through Childhood's fragrant, flowery wonderland
And, entered in the golden realm of Youth,
Fare still a pilgrim toward the copious joys
I savored here yet scarce began to sip;
Yea, with the comrades that I loved so well
Resume the banquet we had scarce begun
When in the street we heard the clarion-call
And each man sprang to arms, ay, even myself
Who loved sweet Youth too truly not to share
Its pain no less than its delight. If prayers
Are to be prayed, lo, here is mine! Be this
My resurrection, this my recompense!

Ode in Memory of the American Volunteers Fallen for France
(To have been read before the statue of Lafayette and Washington in Paris, on Decoration Day,
May 30, 1916.)

I
Ay, it is fitting on this holiday,
Commemorative of our soldier dead,
When with sweet flowers of our New England May
Hiding the lichened stones by fifty years made gray
Their graves in every town are garlanded,
That pious tribute should be given too
To our intrepid few
Obscurely fallen here beyond the seas.
Those to preserve their country's greatness died;

But by the death of these
Something that we can look upon with pride
Has been achieved, nor wholly unreplied
Can sneerers triumph in the charge they make
That from a war where Freedom was at stake
America withheld and, daunted, stood aside.

II

Be they remembered here with each reviving spring,
Not only that in May, when life is loveliest,
Around Neuville-Saint-Vaast and the disputed crest
Of Vimy, they, superb, unfaltering,
In that fine onslaught that no fire could halt,
Parted impetuous to their first assault;
But that they brought fresh hearts and springlike too
To that high mission, and 'tis meet to strew
With twigs of lilac and spring's earliest rose
The cenotaph of those
Who in the cause that history most endears
Fell in the sunny morn and flower of their young years.

III

Yet sought they neither recompense nor praise,
Nor to be mentioned in another breath
Than their blue coated comrades whose great days
It was their pride to share, ay, share even to the death!
Nay, rather, France, to you they rendered thanks
(Seeing they came for honor, not for gain),
Who, opening to them your glorious ranks,
Gave them that grand occasion to excel,
That chance to live the life most free from stain
And that rare privilege of dying well.

IV

O friends! I know not since that war began
From which no people nobly stands aloof
If in all moments we have given proof
Of virtues that were thought American.
I know not if in all things done and said
All has been well and good,
Or if each one of us can hold his head
As proudly as he should,
Or, from the pattern of those mighty dead
Whose shades our country venerates to-day,
If we've not somewhat fallen and somewhat gone astray.
But you to whom our land's good name is dear,
If there be any here
Who wonder if her manhood be decreased,
Relaxed its sinews and its blood less red
Than that at Shiloh and Antietam shed,
Be proud of these, have joy in this at least,

And cry: "Now heaven be praised
That in that hour that most imperilled her,
Menaced her liberty who foremost raised
Europe's bright flag of freedom, some there were
Who, not unmindful of the antique debt,
Came back the generous path of Lafayette;
And when of a most formidable foe
She checked each onset, arduous to stem
Foiled and frustrated them
On those red fields where blow with furious blow
Was countered, whether the gigantic fray
Rolled by the Meuse or at the Bois Sabot,
Accents of ours were in the fierce melee;
And on those furthest rims of hallowed ground
Where the forlorn, the gallant charge expires,
When the slain bugler has long ceased to sound,
And on the tangled wires
The last wild rally staggers, crumbles, stops,
Withered beneath the shrapnel's iron showers:
Now heaven be thanked, we gave a few brave drops;
Now heaven be thanked, a few brave drops were ours."

V
There, holding still, in frozen steadfastness,
Their bayonets toward the beckoning frontiers,
They lie, our comrades, lie among their peers,
Clad in the glory of fallen warriors,
Grim clusters under thorny trellises,
Dry, furthest foam upon disastrous shores,
Leaves that made last year beautiful, still strewn
Even as they fell, unchanged, beneath the changing moon;
And earth in her divine indifference
Rolls on, and many paltry things and mean
Prate to be heard and caper to be seen.
But they are silent, calm; their eloquence
Is that incomparable attitude;
No human presences their witness are,
But summer clouds and sunset crimson-hued,
And showers and night winds and the northern star.
Nay, even our salutations seem profane,
Opposed to their Elysian quietude;
Our salutations calling from afar,
From our ignobler plane
And undistinction of our lesser parts:
Hail, brothers, and farewell; you are twice blest, brave hearts.
Double your glory is who perished thus,
For you have died for France and vindicated us.

Made in the USA
Lexington, KY
12 June 2019